COGNITIVE BEHAVIORAL THERAPY WORKBOOK FOR ADULTS

LEARN SKILLS TO IMPROVE ANXIETY, DEPRESSION, SELF-ESTEEM, AND BECOME MORE POSITIVE, ESCAPE YOUR MENTAL IMPRISONMENT USING CBT

ALIVIA STEPHENS

I dedicate this book to my husband Marc. He has cultivated a supportive environment and made it possible for me to follow my passions in life. He has shown me the real meaning of love and companionship. Also, to my children for being old enough to care for some of their own needs. I hope you all have the freedoms you desire in your bright futures.

CONTENTS

A SPECIAL GIFT TO MY READERS!

Two Quick Hacks To Reframe Your Thoughts To Be More Positive!!!!

Included with your purchase of this book is your own copy of "Change Your Negative Core Beliefs, Find Your Hope" worksheets. These worksheets will assist you in digging into the very necessary work on yourself to gain a more positive outlook on your life. Improve your thinking and self-worth!

Scan the QR code below and let us know which email address to send it to.

For a supportive safe environment of like-minded people, join our CBT Mastermind Support Group on Facebook:

INTRODUCTION: YOU ARE NOT ALONE

Millions of people struggle with sadness, depression, feelings of isolation, anxiety, anger, and chronic pain. All generated by their own thoughts!

We have all the power within us to change this modern loophole of helplessness. This is called a cognitive distortion, a thought that is stubborn in the sense that it has existed inside of you for a very long time, a thought that is maladaptive, warped, but stubborn and ingrained.

We all need those counter thoughts—positive, uplifting, juicy thoughts—that become our reality when we challenge the false narrative we've been living. We sometimes struggle trying to figure out "who we are", to the point of obsession—when the truth is, we are already whole. The problem lies in the fact that we do not *believe* that we are.

When chronic stress, anxiety, depression, and other problems reach severe levels, this warrants serious attention, and this book should be paired with professional help.

However, Cognitive Behavioral Therapy (**CBT**) can be done with or without the help of a therapist and can be combined with other methods.

In *Cognitive Behavioral Therapy Workbook for Adults: Learn Skills To Improve Anxiety, Depression, Self-Esteem, And Become More Positive, Escape Your Mental Imprisonment Using CBT*, I will help you strengthen your confidence and lead you to a more loving relationship with yourself. While you can use this with a therapist, this workbook is meant to serve as a tool *for you*. By using it, you can learn how to become your own therapist by adopting the strategies of CBT that you will learn about in the following chapters.

WHO IS THE AUTHOR?

My name is Alivia, and I am a Certified Alcohol and Drug Counselor. With this workbook, I intend to share the comprehensive skills of CBT so that you can end the self-imprisonment that has held you back from enjoying life and fulfilling your true potential.

Growing up, I struggled with intrusive thoughts. I would think, "I'm not wanted," often feeling 'weirder' than other kids. When I was in elementary school, I'd walk into class thinking, "I hope everyone leaves me alone today." Because I thought this way, from a very young age, I believed that I was worth less than everyone around me. My thoughts consisted of me telling myself that I wasn't "good enough."

I distanced myself from my peers because of how different I felt from them. I remember having a substitute teacher one day in kindergarten, and I thought she was so beautiful. The class was sitting in a reading circle, and I just gazed up at her, wishing I looked like her. I didn't like my appearance in kindergarten!

The negative thoughts about myself continued throughout elementary and on to middle school. Of course, I had no concept of self-love at that age, and I was utterly clueless as to how to feel better about myself. It felt like my entire existence was contingent on who accepted me—especially boys. The more I told myself I was worthless; the more these intrusive thoughts led me to harmful behaviors. By the age of thirteen, I was deep in a lifestyle of self-harm fueled by addictive behaviors. I engaged in criminal behavior and began using methamphetamine. This lifestyle progressed into a full-blown addiction, and by nineteen I was using any drug I could get my hands on.

When I entered recovery, I struggled with social anxieties, severe mania, and *Body-Focused Repetitive Behaviors (BFRBs)*, such as skin picking. I had tried therapy before, but always left feeling unsatisfied, and frustrated. I did, however, know that I already gained a great sense of satisfaction in helping others. I realized that I wanted to continue on my journey of recovery, as I began focusing my energy towards psychotherapy research in 2015. While enrolled in the Psychology program at Grand Canyon University, I learned more about how to teach others about therapy. I gained an even greater understanding of CBT when I began training to become an Alcohol and Drug Counselor. As I learned what it was and how it could be used to help others, and practicing CBT myself, a beautiful transformation took place: my own obsessive, intrusive thoughts began to wither away.

What is the best way to learn something?

According to brain expert Jim Kwik, the best way to teach yourself something is to learn it with the intention of teaching others.

When I set out to learn so that I could teach, that is when I really understood the fundamentals of CBT and how to put it into practice. The mindset of self-hate and worthlessness I'd been living in my whole life finally began to crumble, and I began gaining a deeper sense of awareness that led to discovering my own value.

What happens when your beliefs about yourself and the world begin to change?

Your behavior will change, too. This means that as you begin seeing the world differently; the ways that you interact with it will change as well. Instead of walking into a room ridden with social anxieties, I now walk into a room knowing my own intentions. I know who I am now, and what I'm capable of. I use anchoring, cognitive restructuring, and breathing relaxation to create my ideal reality. These are just a few strategies of CBT that we will dive into more deeply in the following chapters.

Today, I have been in recovery for almost ten years, and have worked in the field of addiction for seven. I have been teaching CBT practices to hundreds of clients. Helping others achieve the knowledge and strength to practice CBT profoundly matters to me, because of the experiences that led me to this field in the first place.

What you're going to learn in this book is what helped me find a true sense of acceptance of myself, and end the self-harming behavior I'd been engaging with most of my life.

WHAT IS THE PURPOSE OF THIS BOOK?

I am writing this book because I have experienced a great deal of pain through self-deprecating thinking and reliance on addiction, and I want to share my knowledge in the hopes of helping others change too. My work aims to help others overcome their maladaptive beliefs and self-limitations. The goal is not to just simply clear your mind, but to also become aware of what ignites your thoughts and feelings, so that you don't allow them to have power over you.

The ultimate goal is for you to begin changing your **core beliefs**, because at the end of the day, they are what determines how you approach life.

Expect to find other pertinent terms like this in **bold text**, which indicates that their definitions can be found in the glossary at the end of this book. As for the objectives you can expect to learn about, they are listed below.

Goals and Objectives

- Identify negative core beliefs and self-limiting thoughts.
- Change your personal and world-view.
- Learn how to maintain your positive changes.
- Learn how to be confident in your life decisions.
- Become your own "CBT Therapist" by learning behavioral practices.
- Better communicate your needs to friends and family.
- Learn how to not be attached to outcomes.
- Release the responsibility of other people's behavior.
- Learn that when people react rather than respond, that it is not your fault, and not your problem to fix!
- Find out how to become aware of your thoughts and emotions, and how they drive your behavior.
- Learn how to change your behavior in order to change your life.

CBT requires consistent effort because it can take time to show results. The knowledge and exercises here will help you begin practicing CBT strategies. If you want positive results, you must maintain a continued desire for self-improvement in order to sustain results.

Set Your Intentions

Please note: If you are reading this workbook through Kindle, other eBook readers, or audio, you will need a pen and paper handy while you work through this book! You can also visit my website at www.awakenyourmindlive.com and there are PDF worksheets under the resources tab. Otherwise, there will be spaces for you to write directly in the book.

To help guide you through this interactive workbook, it will be good to set an intention now by answering (if you can) these questions:

1. What core beliefs are you hoping to change with CBT?

✎...

2. What place do you hope to arrive at once you're able to learn these strategies?

✎...

3. Why do you want to change your thoughts and behavior?

✎...

1

AWAKENING YOUR MIND

Positive Affirmation: I am enough, and I do my best.

Before we talk about the exercises and strategies available to develop and maintain a CBT practice, first, a little history. In this chapter you will learn about the origin as well as the purpose of CBT. You will also learn about the strategies used in CBT practices. Cognitive Behavioral Therapy is for more than your mental health—your mental health determines the capacity of your physical health. This chapter will help you recognize the importance of considering the mind and body as *one being*, not as separate, opposite, or solitary methods of experiencing your world.

"Stoics believed truth is rooted in natural law, and that aligning one's thoughts and expectations with natural order will promote well-being and protect against unnecessary emotional pain" (Mathews, 2015). What this means is that the Stoics believed going against the natural laws of the world is the primary cause of suffering.

Psychologist Albert Ellis established the first cognitive-behavioral therapy called the *Rational Emotive Behavioral Therapy (REBT)*. Ellis used REBT to indicate that emotional and behavioral issues could be treated by identifying lies or disruptions in our belief system. He termed this treatment "cognitive restructuring", a CBT tool still used today to treat problems and disorders. Ellis surmised his ideas from Stoic philosopher, Epictetus. Epictetus thought that our interpretations of events affected us more than the events themselves. He said we are disturbed by events only due to how we view them. When our interpretations are untrue and unrealistic, this goes against the nature of the event and that is when we suffer.

Fast forward to the 1960s, when psychoanalyst Dr. Aaron T. Beck came to be known as "the father of Cognitive Behavior Therapy" (The Beck Institute for Cognitive Behavior Therapy, n.d.-a). This is due to his research on the inner workings of depression: His theory was based on the notion that underlying negative beliefs were linked to failure and loss. These were what conceptualized the illness. This was

ment plans for each study. He was able to help his patients learn how to pinpoint and evaluate their thoughts. The result was that his patients were able to view themselves and the world realistically, without their thoughts being clouded by false information. They felt better and, in turn, behaved better.

The three pillars of Stoicism are still inherent in CBT today: *logic, acceptance,* and *control,* which you will understand as you continue reading. According to Dr. Davis Burns, CBT is the Gold Standard in helping individuals.

Subjective Lens

A subjective lens is the unique lens through which we, as individuals, view the world. We experience and behave the way we do according to what each of us considers to be our absolute truths. An absolute truth is defined as being an "inflexible reality", meaning one that we believe to be factual.

An example of an absolute truth would be saying, "The sky is blue." Most people would likely agree with this statement. However, according to NASA, the sky only *appears* blue due to the phenomenon called **Rayleigh scattering.** The scattering is **electromagnetic radiation**; light energy travels in waves, and when our eyes recognize the color blue, it is because the particles are of a much smaller wavelength, and these shorter wavelengths correspond to our eyes as blue hues.

IS IT RIGHT FOR ME?

Beck's theory taught us that our automatic thoughts are caused by an event or situation that we believe to be impactful. I call these *activating events,* and they can be just about anything, from repeated neglect and disregard from a parent, to going into the grocery store and having a negative experience (anxiety or panic attack, etc.).

Beck's theory is laid out below:

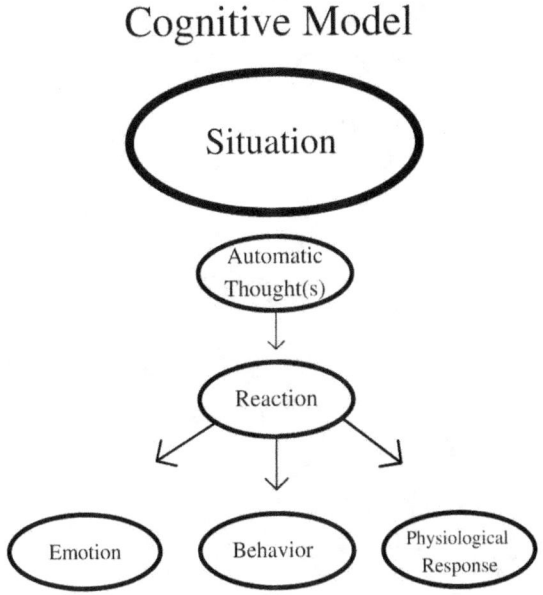

Cognitive Model

mentions that as human beings, we aren't destined to feel or create fear. Our brains are designed to keep us from doing such things, because they're actually designed to keep us safe.

In line with Aaron Beck's findings, the contemporary theory behind CBT attests that:

- Unhelpful ways of thinking contribute to psychological issues.
- Learned behavioral patterns that are unhealthy contribute to psychological issues.
- These problems can be nurtured through healthy coping mechanisms, in order to relieve suffering.

This is further laid out in the CBT Triangle.

The CBT Triangle

The basics of the CBT Triangle:

- **Situations** are any time something happens in your life.
- **Thoughts** are your interpretations of those situations.

For example: If a stranger looks at you with an angry expression, you could think: "Oh no, what did I do wrong?" or, "Maybe they are having a bad day."

- **Emotions** are feelings or states of mind, such as happy, sad, angry, or worried. Emotions can have physical components as well as mental, such as low energy when feeling sad, or a stomachache when nervous.

- **Behaviors** are your physical, verbal, or emotional responses to a situation. Behaviors include actions, such as saying or doing something (or choosing not to say or do something).

The CBT Triangle shows us how thoughts, emotions, and behaviors affect one another. This means changing your thoughts will change how you feel and change your behavior.

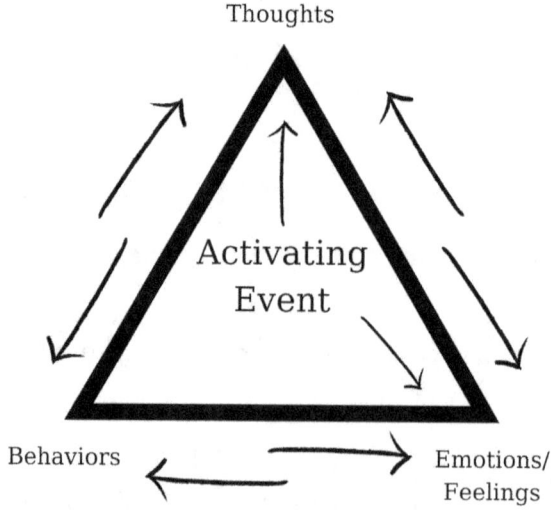

Thoughts

Activating Event

Behaviors

Emotions/ Feelings

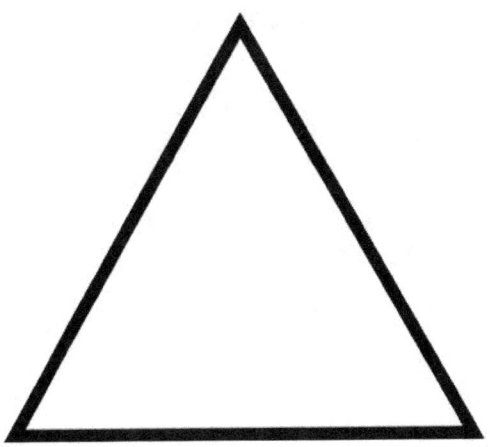

Try This: Now it's your turn to use the CBT Triangle!

- In the center of the triangle above, write an "activating event" that sticks out to you. This could be anything you know that triggered certain unpleasant thoughts, feelings, and behaviors for you.
- After writing in your activating event, go ahead and write on the outside of the triangle the thoughts, emotions/feelings, and behaviors you are able to pinpoint based on the event. This is a chance for you to understand how your thoughts, emotions/feelings, behaviors are all influenced by one another.

15. Mindfulness Meditation
16. Relaxation and Stress Reduction Techniques

WHAT DOES CBT TREAT?

Our **Genetic Predisposition** accounts for about 30% of the health outcomes that our genetics passed down, through physiology and environment. That means there are about 70% open to other factors, and CBT methods can even improve our health. This includes our ability to prevent and manage chronic diseases in our physiology.

Keep in mind that you **do not need a medical diagnosis in order to receive the benefits of CBT**.

It can help anyone with:

- grieving
- ongoing conflicts
- managing intense emotions like sadness, fear, and anger
- managing the symptoms or preventing mental health setbacks
- improving communication skills
- dealing with physical health
- establishing assertiveness
- resolving the effects of trauma

Other forms of depression include:

- **Persistent Depressive Disorder (Dysthymia)**
- **Psychotic Depression**
- **Postpartum Depression**
- **Seasonal Affective Disorder**
- **Bipolar Disorder**

Anxiety

According to the National Institute of Mental Health, anxiety is defined as "a feeling of fear, dread, and uneasiness. It might cause you to sweat, feel restless and tense, and have a rapid heartbeat" (NIMH, 2021). Anxiety is a common response to stress or triggering situations/thoughts. Anxiety can also be an effect of cognitive distortions.

Types of anxiety/ anxiety disorders include:

- **Generalized Anxiety**
- **Panic Disorder**
- **Post-Traumatic Stress Disorder (PTSD)**
- **Social Anxiety**
- **Obsessive-Compulsive Disorder**

Ruminating

'Ruminating' is when you focus on negative situations to an excessive degree. This is most common when someone focuses on their depression symptoms, which just prolongs

practices for relaxing. We can also work on anger by recognizing when we have a negative 'anchor' or attachment to an event, behavior, or place in our body.

Chronic Pain

Chronic pain is consistent or constant pain that persists far longer than it should. This could include any pain that continues past the typical recovery rate. It can occur on and off in someone's life, but the cycle is repeated and can get progressively worse without treatment. Conditions such as *Chronic Pain Syndrome (CPS)* or fibromyalgia can develop over time or suddenly. These have no known cure, only methods to mitigate and reframe the pain—like CBT.

Chronic pain is common, especially headaches, arthritis, back pain, other chronic pain, and musculoskeletal pain. Chronic pain and chronic stress can interact in a vicious cycle. Most of the CBT methods mentioned earlier can help with chronic pain—distraction and relaxation can be particularly helpful.

Addiction

Addiction, also known as *Substance Use Disorder (SUD)*, is a condition in which a person abuses a substance, resulting in harmful effects. People who abuse substances most often struggle with abusing illicit drugs, nicotine, alcohol, and prescription medications. Addiction can harm a person's day-to-day life, often destroying it completely, as addictions can become all-consuming.

replace these thoughts with positive ones that make you feel good, and inspire hopefulness.

CBT can also help with:

- **sleep disorders**
- **trichotillomania**
- **procrastination**
- **ADD/ADHD**
- **obsessive-compulsive disorder (OCD)**
- **bipolar disorders**
- **eating disorders**
- **addiction**
- **post-traumatic stress disorder (PTSD)**
- **phobias**
- **schizophrenia**
- **autism spectrum disorder**
- **traumatic brain injuries (TBI)**

BENEFITS OF CBT

What are the benefits of CBT?

- learning to change your beliefs about yourself
- preventing addiction relapses
- dealing with pain management
- coping with grief
- managing anger
- controlling anxiety

This means that we can also be a completely different person in the future. But it depends on you, and into which direction you are going to steer your boat.

Over time, CBT will begin to really take effect in your life. Depending on the individual, treatment can take anywhere from a few weeks up to a few months before you really start seeing results. Don't let this discourage you; it took time to dig this rut, and it will take time to climb out. Remember that you are not alone in this process, and everything takes time, including healing your mental and physical health.

Time is the coin of your life. It is the only coin you have, and only you can determine how it will be spent. Be careful lest you let other people spend it for you.

— CARL SANDBURG

2

BEGINNING YOUR PRACTICE

Positive Affirmation: Mistakes are opportunities to learn.

The ultimate goal of CBT is to gain the ability to change our core beliefs. How do we do this? Refer back to the CBT Triangle. Our thoughts influence our feelings, and our feelings influence our behavior—this also works the other way around.

In this chapter, you'll learn how to analyze your cognition process to better understand how you feel and behave. We'll discuss how that process creates cognitive distortions. You'll also learn about how those **distortions** create and affect your thought patterns.

distortions are thought patterns causing us to see the world inaccurately.

Remember: Cognitive distortions are almost always negative and irrational.

Reinforced often, and they can cause or increase anxiety and relationship difficulties (if they weren't already the cause), and severely deepen depression symptoms or disorders. Cognitive distortions are upheld primarily as coping mechanisms rather than preferred ways of thinking. They can help us cope with adverse life events, making them a sort of survival strategy.

Below are the many types of cognitive distortions. As common as they are however, they are still irrational and if not addressed, they will cause long-term damage to your health.

▷ **Black and White Thinking**

Having *Black and White Thinking* is when you only experience extremes and dichotomies—seeing things "in black and white," instead of varying shades of gray. It is also known as "polarized thinking". You may even use some of these words yourself:

- always
- never
- impossible
- perfect

▷ **Catastrophizing**

This cognitive distortion leads people to assuming the absolute worst about a situation, especially when they are faced with the unknown. Catastrophizing takes ordinary worries and heightens them to an unbearable level.

For example: Say your partner doesn't arrive on time to your date. When you catastrophize, you begin to fear that your partner hasn't arrived because maybe they were in an accident, or worse, they never planned to show at all.

It's all too easy to deduce catastrophizing to be overreacting or being hysterical, but people with this distortion are reacting this way most likely because of a repeated event in their life that caused negative feelings.

Catastrophizing is often a result of chronic pain, anxiety, depression, PTSD, and especially childhood trauma. These are only a few factors that cause a person to always fear the worst and exaggerate the stressful situations they already deal with. CBT is effective at targeting this distortion by addressing your thought and behavioral patterns so that you can replace irrational thoughts and replace them with realistic ones.

▷ **Overgeneralization**

People that overgeneralize situations reach a conclusion about an event before it has arrived. They extend a negative thought to an even bigger extreme.

to chill, I feel guilty about it later, as if I should have been productive instead. By practicing mindfulness, which you'll learn about later, I've been able to go easier on myself and appreciate moments of down-time without being too hard on myself.

▷ Unqualifying

When you believe that a good thing somehow "doesn't really count" in your larger pattern of failure or negativity. Also known as "Discounting the Positive" this cognitive distortion overshadows positives with false negatives by invalidating the good completely.

For example: I guess I survived the speech I gave—but even broken clocks are right twice a day, and I still messed this part up! Or: Someone compliments you by saying "You're so beautiful, I love your hair," and you unqualify it by saying, "Thanks, but I have really bad acne right now."

This cognitive distortion is also responsible for feelings of hopelessness because you have a total lack of faith in yourself and your life to produce positive results.

▷ Jumping the Gun

This means you are taking barely any or no information and leaping to grandiose conclusions. You fixate on an even bigger and broader negative thought you got from a negative experience. You do this two ways:

▷ Emotional Facts

When you assume your negative thoughts reflect the truth and are in fact reality. Also known as "Emotional Reasoning", this cognitive distortion is based on judging everything based on your emotions.

For example: I felt flustered and humiliated, therefore, I must have been acting in an embarrassing way.

Based on how you felt, you determined the nature of your behavior even if you weren't acting that way at all. Another way of seeing this would be when you are getting ready to perform in a play and because you are so nervous, you believe you performed poorly. In actuality you might have been great, but your emotions keep you from seeing that. Especially due to the high emotional aspect of this distortion, anxiety and depression are high on the list of effects.

▷ "Should Have" Statements

When you beat yourself up for not doing or saying things differently. You see through a lens that tells you there is a way you "should" and "should not" be behaving. If this applies to you, you are probably very anxious or worrisome most of the time.

For example: I should've kept my mouth shut or I should have made this for dinner instead.

By thinking there is a way you "should" be acting, you most likely wind up feeling like a failure most of the time which

could also appear when you blame others for things while ignoring other factors.

Mind Traps

Do any of these apply to you? That's what CBT is for, to change this negative, harmful thinking.

We can all relate to the idea that we are or have been inherently bad. If so, then what is the point in trying to live a healthy life? What do I have to offer the world then? This is what I call a **mind trap!**

Cognitive distortions are comfortable ways of convincing ourselves what we think is true, when actually they are lies being created by the pain of trauma. They are also created from lack of self-reflection and the inability to differentiate your thoughts from fiction. If you believe you are less than, then that's how you'll feel.

How do we squash the lies our mind tells us?

People tend to spend a lot of time feeling alone in today's society, prompting them to also feel deeply misunderstood. Well, I'm here to let you know that you're not alone. It's important to keep in mind that these types of embedded, cognitive distortions are not created overnight. They have existed in us for a long time, so it's imperative to remember to be gentle with yourself. Try your best, be patient, and forgive yourself, even if you slip back into old patterns.

thoughts, cognitive distortions, and new rational thoughts, in that order). Otherwise, use the spaces below:

Step One: In the space below, write down any *automatic thoughts* you're experiencing. Then, read them aloud several times to really let them sink in.

✎...

Step Two: I want you to label what types of cognitive distortions your *automatic thoughts* fall under. Are they *Black and White Thinking, Jumping the Gun, Personalization,* etc.? Make a mind map if you find that helpful.

✎...

Step Three: Write down your new, *rational* thoughts.

✎...

For example: instead of thinking, "I should have made something else for dinner," you can write, "I made alfredo and watched as everyone around me enjoyed it and all that was on their plate. It was a good meal."

Now, take a minute to analyze your results.

3

CREATING NEW HABITS

POSITIVE AFFIRMATION: I am preparing for my ultimate success.

I want to talk with you about how to successfully establish a healthy treatment for yourself. It's important to know exactly what you want to think and feel in order to be able to change it. Take some time now to do just that! Think about how you would like to behave and function in this world. In this chapter and those to follow, you will gain greater knowledge into the exercises of CBT that you can do on your own.

This is an interactive book. This means that if you are not willing to put in a little work and practice the easy exercises, then you aren't likely to receive the outcomes you're hoping for.

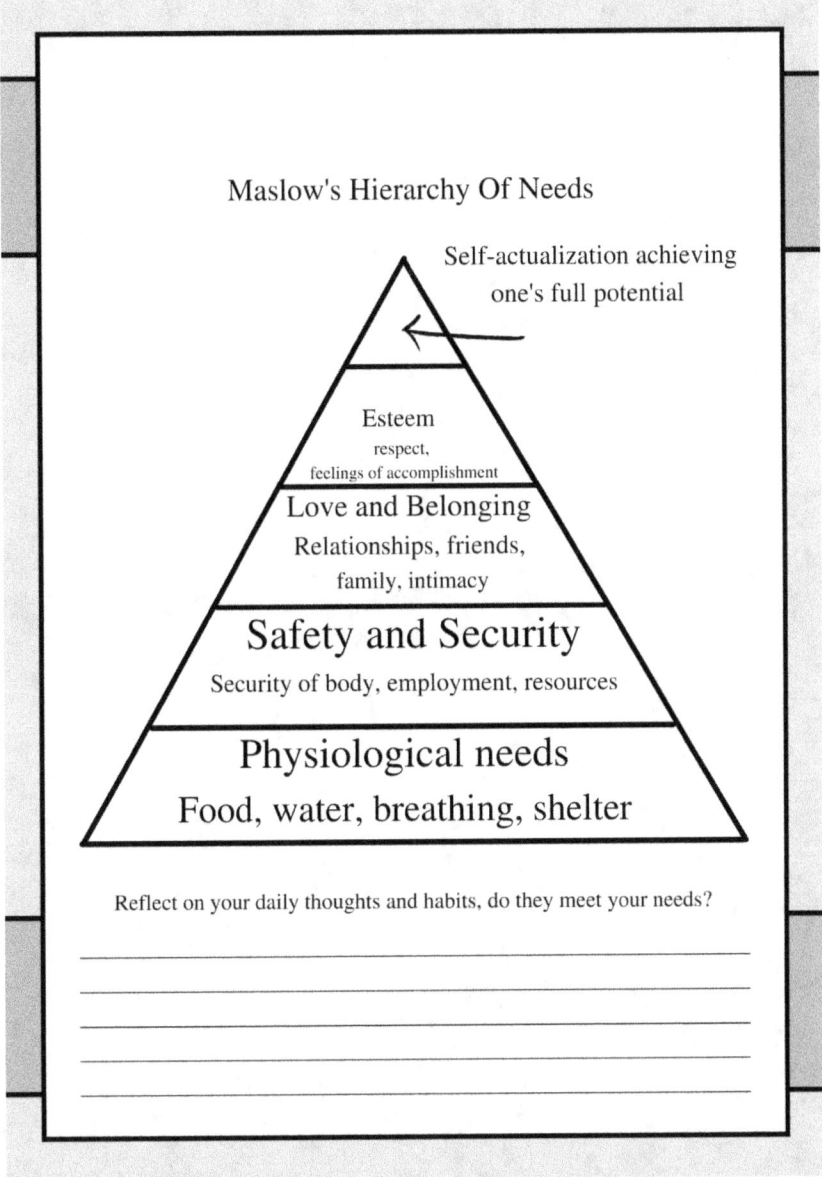

Maslow's Hierarchy Of Needs

Self-actualization achieving one's full potential

Esteem
respect,
feelings of accomplishment

Love and Belonging

Relationships, friends,
family, intimacy

Safety and Security

Security of body, employment, resources

Physiological needs

Food, water, breathing, shelter

Reflect on your daily thoughts and habits, do they meet your needs?

Try This: Go ahead and fill in the spaces of Maslow's Pyramid above. Think about each level and relate them to your own life.

1. Become more present

Maslow described self-actualizing individuals as people who are selflessly present. "Self-actualization [...] means experiencing fully, vividly, selflessly, with full concentration and total absorption," (M. Davis, 2019). This means going about your life without dwelling on the past. When you're present and you focus on your current life, that is a self-actualizing moment in itself. Why? Because when we're present, we're able to understand our experiences.

2. Be aware of the choices you make

From the moment you wake up, you are presented with choices: *Will I go to work today? Will I go back to sleep? What will I have for breakfast?*

Maslow argued that these choices are either "progressive" or "regressive". This means that one choice, such as the choice to get out of bed, will lead you to the next choice. This means that you are moving forward in life and you are satisfying your needs in the process. This is the progressive choice because it encourages growth, whereas a regressive choice could be you feeling too tired so you go back to sleep and you miss work. By making a decision like this, you are choosing to sabotage the second level of needs: safety. Your safety becomes compromised; say you lose your job! You now have a lack of financial security.

"It means making each of the single choices about whether to lie or be honest, whether to steal or not steal at a partic-

tionships, but "being okay with that was something he believed was indispensable for self-actualization" (Bigthink, n.d.).

6. Continuously self-actualize

As you know, working on yourself will never end. It's about satisfying your needs so you can enjoy your growth periods. Self-actualizing includes realizing your abilities every second of every day. What task or skill are you capable of accomplishing right now? People who are self-actualizing are constantly striving to be their best selves.

7. Acknowledge your great experiences

Moments that feel good, these "peak" experiences, are literally moments of self-actualization. This is because in those moments, you are filled with pleasure. It isn't productive to actively search for these moments (and this makes living in the present more difficult). They are to be acknowledged when they happen because reveling in your positive, uplifting moments allows you to feel motivated to continue on this journey.

8. Be prepared to get familiar with psychopathology

Sounds scary, but all this means is that you need to be prepared to confront the most difficult, upsetting aspects of yourself. You have to be willing to challenge who you have been if you want to realize who you are and who you can be. This is a painful process for most, because our defense

Below is an outline of The Reality Model. Challenge yourself to begin this process by keeping these Seven Natural Laws of the model in mind:

1. If the results of my behavior don't meet my needs, then I know there's a false principle in my belief window.
2. The results will take some time to measure.
3. Growth is in the process of changing the principles in my belief window.
4. Deep and unmet needs result in addictive behavior.
5. If my self-worth is based on anything external, I'm in big trouble.
6. As the results of my behavior meet my needs over time, I will begin to experience inner peace.
7. The mind naturally searches for harmony when two opposing beliefs are presented.

The Reality Model

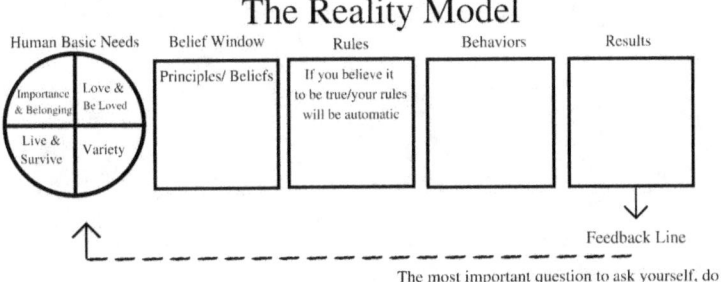

The most important question to ask yourself, do your results meet your needs?

addresses our needs. Based on our belief window, we think "If *this* is true, then *that* will happen". These If-Then Rules we establish for ourselves become a part of our behavioral patterns. The results are what we expected to happen, and when we reach the *feedback* level, we are to examine if our belief window satisfies our needs. If not, then something needs to change.

For example:

- You *need* to be at work by 9am.
- You *believe* that taking the shortcut will get you there on time.
- According to your rules, *if* you take the main streets, *then* you are going to be late because of traffic.
- Your *behavior* looks like you honking at other cars, speeding through lights or back-alleys or missing traffic stops in order not to be late.
- The *results?* Say you just barely make it on time. You're out of breath, full of adrenaline, and now you have to go through work not as put together as you were before.
- *Feedback?* What if rushing like this becomes a habit? What if the shortcut closed next time due to traffic? What if speeding gets you pulled over by a cop?

Remember, your beliefs do not apply to everything and everyone.

Both models work to satisfy these basic human needs and in turn are leading you to make behavioral changes. How? Your belief window is what determines *how* you are going to meet your needs. Meaning, based on your own understanding of yourself and the world and what you believe to be true, that understanding of reality is how you satisfy your needs.

It's not easy to change your beliefs. That's why beginning CBT and approaching The Reality Model requires you to make the commitment of wanting to change the ways you interact with yourself and the world. With consistency, the hard work will benefit you down the line, not just in that moment.

Emotional Triggers

Now I want to talk to you about **emotional triggers**. Emotional triggers can be an object, a person, a memory, or even a sight, sound, taste, or touch that provokes intense emotions. Basically, an emotional trigger is anything that stirs up negative emotions. Some people may think of triggers as those activating events we talked about. This is because both spark past traumas that have been stored in us for so long. Being triggered can often occur abruptly, when you weren't expecting it. Due to this, triggers are usually hard to control. Sometimes they can feel subtle like not knowing why you are irritated suddenly.

Substance abuse can especially aggravate anger triggers.

- **Trauma Triggers:** Trauma triggers are typically associated with PTSD because this type of trigger reminds a person of an extremely negative, painful past. It's especially common in veterans of war and abuse survivors. People who deal with trauma triggers tend to exhibit **avoidance** behavior. This means that they avoid anything and anyone that could set them off. What's also interesting about trauma triggers is that they can spontaneously appear in memories and dreams. People who struggle with this trigger often relive the harmful experience and may show symptoms like vomiting or hyperventilating.

For example: A High Schooler has a fear of water because of a near fatal drowning experience when they were younger. This student has avoided water ever since. In gym class, this student is being told that swimming is mandatory, therefore emotionally triggering them. They might experience anxiety, shaking, or nausea. Being told to swim was an emotional trigger because it reminded them of an extremely negative experience they tried hard not to think about. So, when confronted with a trigger, they started to panic.

This would classify as a trauma trigger, because the students' avoidance of triggering situations acted as their coping mechanism to deal with their traumatic experience. This is related to PTSD.

Triggers Exercise

Try This: Here's an exercise you can try in order to help you iden-tify your emotional triggers.

When you're calm and you feel like you can understand your cognitions, go ahead and take a few minutes to write down the types of signs and signals within your body that you're experiencing in the space below: (*This means noticing if your blood pressure does indeed rise when you're angry, maybe your nostrils flare, or maybe you're like me and you feel like you are clenching your jaw, or make a weird growling noise when you're angry*)

✎...

Ask yourself, what is triggering me to make me feel this way? The result you want is being able to pinpoint that trigger so you can figure out how to respond.

It's helpful to establish at least three key ideas on how you think you're going to manage your anger response (or what-ever negative emotion you're feeling). To do this, think about what is going to make you feel better and allow you to cool off. Write your guesses below:

1. ✎...

A famous example would be Russian physiologist Ivan Pavlov's experiment. He used a stimulus to produce a reaction. In the experiment, Pavlov used dogs to demonstrate that hearing a bell ring would stimulate feelings of hunger. This was done by consistently ringing the bell (stimulus) so that the dogs would learn to associate it with food. "Pavlov found he could eventually just ring the bell and the dogs would start salivating, even though no food was given" (Crowe-Associates, n.d.). The dogs were **conditioned** to think about food and feel hungry at the sound of that bell. In this conditioning experiment, the stimulus was the environmental cue of the bell, and the response was a specific behavior.

More than just environmental cues can provide links between other experiences as well. A specific shirt or painting can inspire specific internal feelings just as the sound of your mother's voice can produce a certain feeling. Feelings spawned from environmental cues can be positive such as hearing a certain song that produces specific feelings of joy or excitement.

The trick with anchoring is switching your response from mindless (twitch, knee jerk, etc.), to one that you choose. You want to choose your anchor based on how good it makes you feel, rather than being anchored in a negative experience. This is one of those strategies that will offer you more self-control.

✎...

For example:

If you are experiencing an anger trigger or you've been able to identify it as one of your problems, you probably want to feel calm and relaxed.

Think of a moment where you were at peace such as a yoga retreat or maybe a day on the beach.

Say you choose a beach memory. Maybe you choose sound as your anchor, in which case your anchor could be the sound of the waves, or seagulls flying by.

Now you close your eyes and use the sound of the waves or seagulls to really take you back to that memory. This is where you begin anchoring yourself in that relaxed feeling.

Go ahead and try this exercise now, and write down what you experienced. As with all skill learning exercises, repeating this anchoring technique is surely a way for you to tackle your triggers head on.

Strategy: Fact-Checking

Fact-checking, like anchoring, is an emotional regulation tool. It allows you to identify what specific emotions you're feeling, and helps you to see the factors that are causing those emotions to rise within you. This strategy will ask you to provide evidence that supports your negative assump-

What events, if any, triggered your emotions?

As mentioned, fact-checking only works if you are able to see what thoughts are opinions, and what are actually facts. The key is identifying what you do and don't have control over. If you do have control or are able to gain it, then you can be able to problem-solve them.

Fact-Checking Exercise

Sometimes our feelings are strong enough to feel like evidence to support our opinions. For instance, "I am so ugly" can feel so real and so true, it's almost impossible to see otherwise. I'm personally guilty of this! I used to say horribly unkind things to myself because I believed them to be true.

When we treat our thoughts as if they're facts, harmful ideas like "I am a horrible person" or "I am so fat" can take root as your cognition pattern. These ideas contribute to our negative feelings of anger, anxiety, insecurity, resentment, etc. However, since we are all seeing through our subjective lens, it's all too easy to see the world as fact versus what is opinion. What makes fact from opinion easy to understand is remembering that facts require evidence in order to be considered fact in the first place.

Try this fact-checking exercise just to see if you can differentiate your opinions from facts. Beside each statement, write fact or opinion.

had an irrational thought process to, where you have problems that have occurred.

This is where you start to recognize what is happening in your life to trigger the emotions that produce problematic thoughts and behaviors.

What happened to make you angry and react irrationally? What happened to make you think that you aren't smart (etc.)?

4

RESTRUCTURING THE MIND AND BODY

POSITIVE AFFIRMATION: All problems have solutions.

Our emotions are our internal GPS system. In this chapter, we're going to dive deeper into learning how to change our core beliefs by discussing how to understand our emotions. We've talked about emotional triggers and have identified two strategies so far to monitor emotions: anchoring and fact-checking. Both addressed inciting events and external factors that influence your emotions, but now we are going to further analyze how to get in touch with the root of our emotions.

We are going to address how to observe your mood so you see how the emotion you're feeling influences your thoughts and behavior. This chapter will also lean into cognitive restructuring. Cognitive Restructuring refers to the general

because you feel numb to your emotions. For others, sometimes a certain physical sensation or thought will be associated with your mood.

The following exercise will help you learn to monitor your moods.

You want to start by setting aside at least a little bit of time each day, so you can reflect on the emotions you're feeling. This can be every day after breakfast, lunch, etc., or even throughout the day—whichever is easiest, as long as you are taking the time to do so. The point is to learn from your emotions by observing and keeping tabs on your emotional experiences.

Strategy: Thought Records

Begin keeping a **thought record**. A thought record is a CBT tool in the form of a journal or log that is used to understand how your thoughts are affecting your feelings and behavior.

- ✎...
- ✎...
- *I got into an argument with my mother. (anger) (embarrassment) (frustration)*
- *This morning I remembered that I owe a late fee on a bill (panic) (worry).*

Step Three: Think about how intense the emotions felt, and rate them on a scale of 1-10, 10 being the highest level of intensity and 1 being the lowest. If it helps, judge the intensity of your emotion by thinking about how you felt.

Before the argument, I felt mildly angry, but during the argument my anger progressed to an extreme level. So, during the argument my anger was definitely at a 10.

Or,

- *I got into an argument with my mother. (anger 10) (embarrassment 7) (frustration 7)*
- *This morning I remembered that I owe a late fee from not paying that bill on time. (panic 8) (worry 10)*
- ✎...
- ✎...
- ✎...

Step Four: Now, see if you can identify the thoughts that appeared during that moment and write them down. You can use a word, sentence, or even describe an image that may

Try and complete a thought record *at least* once a day. The more you do, the more you can become aware of your thoughts and emotions working together. The next step is where you begin working on how to monitor your moods.

Step Five: Using your thought record entries, write down the feelings you noticed and any other physical sensations. *Did you get goosebumps? Did you start sweating or crying?*

- *I got into an argument with my mother. (anger 10) (embarrassment 7) (frustration 7): nostrils flare, racing heartbeat, flushed face*
- *This morning I remembered that I owe a late book fee to the library. (panic 8) (worry 10): dizziness, sweaty palms, nauseous feeling in my throat*
- ✎...
- ✎...
- ✎...

How did this exercise make you feel? I recommend that you try keeping a thought record for at least a week to get the hang of it. Try to track as many thoughts as you can that occur in a negative situation. The more you are able to track your thoughts, it will get easier to check in with your mood.

Strategy: Cognitive Restructuring

Cognitive Restructuring is a CBT skill that touches on the ability to identify inaccurate patterns in cognition. It is meant to help you reshape your thoughts to be more ratio-

your mood. That's not always the case. The best way to achieve this ability is practicing it every day. It should become automatic, a part of your cognition routine. Below are the steps you can take to begin understanding the process of cognitive restructuring:

Step One: Refer back to your thought record.

As previously instructed, think of a situation that made you angry (or sad, distressed, etc.) and write it down. Then write all the thoughts that popped into your head when you started feeling angry. Pay attention to the moments that triggered negative thoughts and feelings. With cognitive restructuring, it's very important to recognize exactly what is in the negative automatic and intrusive thoughts. You can use the space below if needed.

✎...

Step Two: Look at the thoughts you were able to track and choose an automatic one.

Focus on the one you think triggered negative emotions within you and feels most distressing. If that seems too difficult, look at what you've written and find the one that, at the moment, makes you feel the worst. That will tell you which thought gives you the strongest, negative emotion. Let's use all new examples this time:

that it doesn't drag you down or keep you from feeling and behaving positively.

For example, consider this event alone or as part of a thought record:

You're up for a spot on the track team, but a different person from your class was chosen instead. This might make you feel disappointed, a natural response. It might cause you to think "I'm never going to make it on the team now."

Situation: You're up for a spot on the track team, but a different person from your class was chosen instead.

Automatic Thought: "I'm never going to make it on the team now."

Belief: I'm not good at anything.

Take a moment to write down what beliefs you think your automatic thoughts stem from:

✎...

How does a thought like that play a role in your life?

Well, when you believe it, that belief will transfer over to other situations, not just when it comes to making the team. You'll probably feel worse and worse, your disappointment transforming into depression possibly.

2. Think back to the Fact-Checking strategy from Chapter 3.

That strategy asked you to provide evidence that does and does not support your negative assumptions. The point was to differentiate your opinions from actual facts. This same strategy is a helpful tool in learning how to imagine different points of views.

Ask yourself: *What is the evidence that proves my negative thought is right? What evidence goes against my point of view?*

Evidence "Proving" Negative Thought:

✎...

Evidence Against Negative Thought:

✎...

By asking yourself these questions you are learning how to judge the accuracy of your thoughts. If no evidence supports your automatic thought, then you can realize what belief is encouraging that thought and determine why you behave in response to your thoughts and feelings.

For example: Consider the track team example. Evidence you might use to support the thought "I'm never going to make it on the team now" can look like this:

Not all of these are super positive. The point is acknowledging the negative too, such as noticing that you tripped. This is understanding *the logical reason* you didn't make the team. By finding evidence that challenges what you believe to be true, you are turning super negative, distressing moments into ones that are manageable. Doing so, you're not allowing your own negativity to overwhelm you and take over your thought patterns.

If you find yourself having trouble identifying "evidence against", look back at the "evidence proves" list and look for statements that only slightly resemble the truth. Think of answering the "evidence against" question by trying to *defend* the "evidence proves" list.

Is the evidence you are using substantial enough to be true?

This question is key here because you are essentially asking yourself: *Is this just a thought, or is this actually true? What proves it's true? What proves it's false?*

By answering both evidence questions, you are analyzing your thoughts with the intentional purpose of learning how to change your cognition. You're able to understand the situation clearly by determining what evidence actually supports your assumptions and what doesn't.

Something I want you to remember: Simply challenging your negative thoughts is one of the kindest ways you can be towards yourself! This is because you're challenging that

- *He's in a new relationship and is spending all his time with his girlfriend.*
- *He's been away from his phone a lot.*
- *His phone broke and he doesn't know how to reach out to Cara (and that's why he might not be responding too).*
- *John feels like texting Cara out of the blue will bother her* (not an uncommon explanation).
- *Maybe he expects Cara to text first since that's what she always does anyways.*

Some might be more realistic than others, but the point is that Cara can't support her own theory of him possibly hating her, when a million other reasons could explain the silence on his end. By being able to imagine possible explanations that differ from her automatic thoughts, she's gaining the ability to not rely on the truth of those automatic thoughts as much as she once did. Cara will end up feeling better because she isn't placing so much emphasis on the negative ideas that pop up in her thought process.

4. What is the best and worst that could happen?

I mean really, will you survive the negative situation you're thinking of? Have you thought of confronting the problem? What's more likely, the best or worst outcome? Especially in moments of anxiety and fear, it's extremely helpful to identify other possibilities. We tend to fixate on the worst which is why negative thoughts can take over your mindset when really the fixation is what is making you feel bad.

These questions will offer perspective on the worst-case scenario and like finding "evidence against", the situation will feel more manageable.

Cara might answer these questions like this:

- *It will be hurtful to lose a friend and I'll feel really sad, but I'll survive. If it does go bad, I can call my other friend or even a family member to keep me comfortable. A week later I might still feel miserable about the situation, but I'll have had more time to process it. In a month, I might not feel as sad, and I may even stop thinking about it for most of the time. I think in a year I'll have moved on and have made better friends. That will actually work out for me, because I don't want a friend that thinks I'm annoying and would rather not talk to me at all instead of being honest with me.*

Now, let's imagine a fleshed-out example of a best-case scenario that Cara might imagine:

- *John will understand why not reaching out to me would make me feel bad. He might say that he thought he'd be bothering me and now he'll know that isn't the case. Now, he'll reach out more often and I can stop worrying that he hates me and finds me annoying.*

This could definitely be possible as a best-case scenario. Like worst-case scenarios though, the best one typically isn't the

Imagine a friend came to you with the same problem as Cara. What would you tell them? Would you only give them a worst-case scenario? I know you know that it's not easy to get out of your head so you can think clearly, so imagining the situation as if someone you care about was in your place will help you depersonalize the situation and see other perspectives better.

If _____ were in this situation, what would you tell them?

✎…

6. What do I have control of in this situation?

Once you have tried the previous exercises, hopefully you have a clear sense of the whole picture, not just your own point of view. Gaining control over our experiences is ultimately what we want. By looking at the situation and figuring out what you are capable of, you are not only being more present for an upsetting circumstance, but you are actively engaging with this experience. This is what you want rather than allowing your negative thoughts, feelings, and behaviors to run on autopilot.

Ask yourself: *How will I realistically be able to deal with this situation?*

✎…

Why? Because a lot of our stress, worry, and anxiety stems from looking into the unknown. This means that not knowing what could happen is what causes us to think of the worst possible scenarios. And that, my friends, concludes step three.

Step Four: Write a different response

After answering most of these questions you might already feel a little better. Now, really challenge yourself to craft one statement that responds to your automatic thoughts. As I've said, I know it's not easy to simply throw out negative thoughts with positive ones, but allowing a different way of responding to exist alongside your automatic thoughts can help you acknowledge the negative without letting it control you.

Try This: Think of this alternate response as crafting a belief to challenge the one that pushes a negative automatic thought. For the following example, refer back to the track team example:

Automatic Thought: *"I'm never going to make it on the team now."*

✎...

How? Your hand moves according to memory because of the movement required to write the letters of the alphabet. In research from Vargas and Yoon (2004), memory relates to three processes in the brain: **encoding** (the process by which information is put into memory), **storage** (the process by which information is maintained in memory), and **retrieval** (the process by which information is recovered from memory)".

When you write things down, your brain initiates your **encoding** process. Encoding is the process of transferring information to your brain's **hippocampus**—where your brain decides to store information for an extended period of time, or to discard it. Writing things down is also useful because whatever you're writing is occurring in an external storage space, such as the paper you are writing on. Having a physical location for the information helps to materialize the words also making it easier to access at any time.

In a journal, as a list, on a sticky note, or wherever else that is easily accessible—it's especially important to write down your goals. Remember this when you approach the CBT practices to help hold yourself accountable and stay on track.

Strategy: Journaling

Journaling is a classic way of understanding your thoughts. It is helpful to write down the negative and positive thoughts you have so you can vent your emotional experiences. This can help you talk about them too because you are laying out

5

BEGIN TO EMPOWER YOURSELF

POSITIVE AFFIRMATION: I allow myself permission to grow.

Welcome to Chapter 5! If you've made it this far in the workbook, congratulations! That shows you are dedicated to seeing your healing through. Now that we've covered emotional triggers and have gone in-depth as to how you can control your emotions, this chapter will focus on behavior related strategies and how they contribute to changing our core beliefs.

You have a little bit of an idea about the primary aims of CBT like how to alter self-defeating thoughts, tame overwhelming emotions, and control ineffective behavior. Some of these strategies you will learn about in this chapter are forms of cognitive restructuring because changing behavior requires you to change your thinking around that behavior.

emotion may also seem negative because it can trigger anger and sadness, but fear actually has a very useful purpose. It is encouraged due to perceived threats, which we need in order to know when we're in danger. Fear is your body's way of telling you you're not safe. This triggers your **flight-or-flight** response, which is controlled by our *Reticular Activating System (RAS)*.

I mentioned the RAS in Chapter 1 in relation to our subjective lenses. "The groupings of neurons that together make up the RAS are ultimately responsible for attention, arousal, modulation of muscle tone, and the ability to focus" (Arguinchona & Tadi, 2021). This shows how our brain stem associates with our subjective lens because our beliefs tell us what to be afraid of. This is because our fight-or-flight response system helps us respond to our external environments, and when according to our subjective lens, we physically respond based on the cognitive distortions we all possess. For instance, when an encounter causes anxiety or fear, that feeling will tell our body how to respond such as to run or to fight back at whatever is causing us to feel fearful.

In the podcast, *Two for You*, they describe the RAS as the tool that's connecting our subconscious with the conscious part of the brain (Rothstein & Stromme, n.d.). You can think of the RAS as a sort of 'filter' for your brain. This filter is your brain's way of protecting itself, because if we didn't have this filter, there would be way too much information flooding our consciousness throughout the day.

world that are irrational. As you know, not everything we believe is true, and when we don't realize that, our beliefs can cause us a lot of suffering.

Strategy: Self-Monitoring

This strategy can be a helpful way of tracking your behavior. Because we tend to excessively overestimate or underestimate the severity of our behaviors, keeping track of your behavior is to:

1. Understand how often the behavior is engaged.
2. Identify what patterns in an individual's life are leading them to their harmful behavior.

Self-monitoring is especially helpful if you struggle with substance abuse. This is because you are able to see not only how often you use, but you'll be able to understand what makes you want to use and the intensity behind your urges.

Strategy: Exposure Therapy

This strategy asks you to slowly expose yourself to things that make you uncomfortable, perhaps things you fear. This can get a bit sticky if you fear something that is actually threatening, so DO NOT put yourself in (literal) harm's way. Exposure Therapy is often effective in treating anxiety disorders. Individuals expose themselves to situations that trigger anxiety until they eventually become desensitized to those situations.

of fear? Or anxiety? Activity scheduling is a productive way to establish good habits. It's meant to help you increase behaviors you know you need to do to stay on track of changing your behavior. Once you have been able to identify the behaviors you need to change, your goals can become tackling the new behaviors you know will help you with your problems. Here are some methods you can try:

- **Put it in the calendar**

Writing the helpful new behaviors you've adapted into your calendar increases the likelihood of you actually accomplishing it. This is especially helpful if you procrastinate, or if you have difficulty engaging with other people and fun activities. Getting used to using a calendar can also help you keep track of things you need to get done. Doing so can help hold yourself accountable so that you stop putting things off and avoiding responsibilities. You're more likely to follow through when you've already scheduled what you need to get done. Once the burden of decision is gone, you may be more likely to follow through.

- **Make a Pleasant Activities List**

Spending your time doing pleasant activities helps you feel less stressed, and helps you become emotionally healthier. Take some time to build your list of pleasant activities that you feel you are going to enjoy, and divide them into the

- Improve your **problem-solving skills.**
- Become familiar with the difficult situations you often find yourself in so you can trust how you respond instead of just reacting.
- Your **communication** and **social skills** will improve.
- You will feel more empowered because you know what you are and aren't capable of in a situation, knowledge that will offer you more control.

Strategy: Successive Approximation

This strategy is really helpful if you have difficulty finishing a task. You may start it, but whether you feel overwhelmed or not knowledgeable enough for the task, you just don't seem to finish it. That's why successive approximation works by doing only one step at a time. This means that you're building up to facing an overwhelming situation. Unlike role playing, you will tackle your stressors in increments rather than all at once. You will be able to focus on what is more achievable for you by starting with one step (smaller aspect of the stressor) and building up to the main event. With each successive step, you will build upon the first and continue learning how to deal with the stressor. By making your own capacity to deal with situations the focus, you are better able to gain confidence in these stressful moments you find yourself in.

talking about every single detail of *why* you don't feel good about that choice.

✎...

Ask yourself: *How does unpacking my bad choices help me?*

This is an opportunity to think about what positive choices you can make instead of the negative ones that may be running on auto-pilot. Remember, this is all about regaining control of your cognition so you can have an awareness of your behavior.

6

GROWING INTO YOUR BEST SELF

POSITIVE AFFIRMATION: I am unique and I am empowered.

You've made it to Chapter 6! Take a deep breath and congratulate yourself for being here. You've just finished learning about the strategies that can help you step beyond your fears and into a headspace where *you* control how comfortable you are in a situation. We know fear can be as healthy an emotion as it can be unhealthy, but we're learning how to disengage with the latter.

In this chapter, we're going to become familiar with another key step in learning how to empower yourself: learning to navigate interpersonal relationships. In addition, we're going to continue learning how to gain the strength to confront your fears by checking out the reasons we often struggle with communication. We're going to talk about the various

know how to communicate in order to get your needs met. Let's go through the different communication styles:

1. Assertive Communication

It's thought of as the most effective communication style because it is direct. A person communicating with this style has confidence that allows them to state their convictions in a way that exhibits self-assurance but without belittling the other person(s).

This kind of communicator uses a lot of "I" statements. This person has no shame in owning their feelings and behaviors, speaking very clearly what the "I" wants and needs. However, this communicator is still able to actively listen to another person. They're calm and sensitive to other points of views while not losing track of their own. This means that an assertive communicator seeks balance in a conversation rather than aiming to overpower the exchange.

If you want to become an assertive communicator, try these tips:

- Learn to say "no", when you don't want to say "yes".
- Make eye contact.
- Use more "I" statements. You want to speak from a place of confidence.
- Be vocal about expressing your needs, but be sure to do so while still considering the needs of those you are trying to communicate with.

- Check the hostility by examining your body language! This is one of the biggest reasons communication can be difficult. An aggressive communicator's immediate reaction is most often threatening, making productive conversation impossible. When you respond, see how your body language and tone changes. Don't intimidate by getting too close and dominating the physical space. Instead, step back, take a deep breath, and lower your tone. This will provoke a calmer, productive exchange.

- An aggressive communicator wants to seem confident, but really they are in defense mode. Their self-assurance comes from undervaluing another person's feelings. Work on this by thinking about how your behavior is being displayed and how it is affecting whoever you're speaking to.

3. Passive Communication

A passive communicator is the opposite of both the assertive and aggressive communicator. A person with this kind of style shows indifference and yields to those around them when it comes to communicating. They don't do well in expressing their feelings and needs, and usually only allow others to express themselves. Because of this, their behavior leads to a lot of misunderstanding, resentment, and bottling of emotions. For other people talking with a passive communicator, it will be easy because the passive person

4. Passive-Aggressive Communication

With this style, a person that communicates passive-aggressively never shows their true feelings, and because of this, they tend to build up a lot of resentment. This resentment bubbles over and shows itself by the person acting out in indirect ways that subtly express anger. This is because a passive-aggressive usually feels so powerless internally, that they literally find it too hard to say how they're really feeling, so they just bottle everything up until they explode. Basically, on the surface this person is passive, but below the surface aggression is brewing.

A passive-aggressive communicator mutters under their breath instead of being direct and addressing another person head on. In fact, this kind of communicator even has difficulty acknowledging their emotions making it even harder to express their anger and sadness in order to find a solution. Oftentimes they'll deny that there's even a problem to address in the first place. This contradicts their behavior however, because this communicator typically resorts to using the silent treatment or using their body language to show how they feel even though they are saying the opposite. Like aggressive communication, this style is not healthy, and should be worked on.

when they are communicating. This is often shown through **gaslighting.**

Someone communicating in a manipulative manner appears insincere, and has a tendency to belittle you in a conversation. As can be expected, once you realize you've been communicating with a person like this, future interactions will be affected. Occasionally, this kind of communication can be useful if you're in a position of trying to diffuse a situation, but often it just leads to a lot of clashing and patronization. This kind of communicator is very aware of their needs and motivations, they just struggle to get there honestly and with a clear interest in another person's needs.

If you want to work on not communicating this way, try these tips:

- Be direct about your needs instead of hiding your true feelings. This starts with accepting that your way is not always the best way and that you're only hurting yourself by lying.
- Know that being a manipulative communicator is and will continue to damage your relationships. No one responds well to this behavior, and will most likely result in a lot of people around you feeling a lot of resentment and anger because they're aware of your motivation to deceive.
- Do not play off other people's emotions. Instead, stick to the facts in a given situation rather than

I am with people. I'm attentive and empathetic, so the passive communicator in me is staying silent in the hopes that the other person is being as attentive to my problems as I am to theirs. But no one is a mind reader, right? Personally, learning to be a more assertive communicator has been the only thing that's allowed me to have a voice and not feel silenced or ignored.

Take a moment to think about which communication style you adhere to: assertive, aggressive, passive, passive-aggressive, or manipulative. Afterwards in the space below, write down the traits of each style that you know you have, and the behaviors you exhibit:

✎...

Four Forms of Communication

To learn how to adjust your communication style to be helpful for you and the people you communicate with, let's take a minute to learn about the four communication techniques that we present through each communication style:

1. Visual

You probably use visual forms of communication because we do live in the digital era after all. From Instagram, to Twitter, Tik Tok and more, communicating through images is the norm.

ment, right? It's common for most people to not be aware when they react non-verbally. This is because it is displayed using facial expressions, body language, and eye contact.

You can work on how you communicate through each style simply by knowing the intentions behind your voice. What do you *mean* to say? Are you showing that?

Think about how you communicate through each style. Are you more verbal? Non-verbal? Are visuals your thing? Or, like this book, do you communicate in written forms?

In the space below, record the forms you have been able to pinpoint and list the forms you think would be beneficial for you in the future.

✎...

Connection

Most of the strategies in this workbook so far have been related to changing your cognition so you can learn to behave better towards not only yourself, but the people in your life. So, if we are learning how to address the people and problems that cause us to feel negatively, then knowing how to effectively communicate is a valuable source for creating meaningful connections with yourself and others. Not only that, but while we're trying to understand our automatic and intrusive thoughts, it helps to know how to change them if we can communicate how we truly feel.

about interpersonal relationships, then boundaries can be understood as the limits that indicate how close you allow others to get to you.

Why are boundaries important?

Sometimes we need to draw lines within our relationships! "Boundaries are one of the measures of relationship health. As such, they can contribute to your relationships with your partner, children, family, and friends in positive or negative ways" (Very Well Mind 2021). This means that boundaries have a strong influence in how we communicate and relate to others. We can't both prioritize other people's feelings while also setting boundaries. They completely contradict. So before you even try to establish healthy boundaries, keep in mind that doing so is you putting yourself first! You can't continue to put everyone else first if you want to work on a more loving relationship with yourself.

Having compassion for others is an invaluable characteristic, but caring too much for others can feel draining at some point because you aren't reserving any of that positive energy for yourself. Trust me, I know. This is kind of sounding like the passive and passive- aggressive communicators right?

Does this apply to you?

At some point, you need to make a choice, continue to live in others' shadow by not respecting your needs and desires, or work on changing those core beliefs so you can *believe* that

tionships have a sense of closeness because they require a certain level of trust.

Why? Because if we want to openly communicate, being comfortable with vulnerability is the only way.

Setting boundaries is just about letting others be close to you but in a healthy way that doesn't push you or the other party into codependency or disadvantage on either side. Close interpersonal connections are about respecting one another's needs, but also their limits. Healthy boundaries can help you be independent while helping you to communicate better.

Don't get me wrong. Not everyone will respond to your boundaries. These are the times that people should be kept at arm's length because their lack of respect can continue to cause you to feel negatively. When we can have healthy boundaries, we can continue to grow while also having close people in your life to help you.

Try setting boundaries by repeating these mantras daily, from Melody Beattie's book, *The Language of Letting Go:*

Try This: During your next conversation, practice your listening skills by not focusing on how you're going to respond yet. When it's your turn, first take 5–10 seconds to really absorb what you're hearing so you can choose how to respond before your emotions choose for you.

Strategy: Problem-Solving

This is a good strategy to have in your back pocket for many areas of your life. Probably because of all the hurdles we encounter everyday from finances, career, relationships— you name it. It's just a part of life. Learning how to find solutions is the most effective way to solve a problem rather than reacting on auto-pilot. Problem-solving can also look like cognitive restructuring, because you are breaking down a problem and being realistic and rational about trying to solve it.

1. Define the problem

We all react to life in our own unique way (you remember the subjective lens right?). You may avoid problems, or react irrationally, compulsively, possibly with a slight or major hint of aggregation.

Clearly describe the problem at hand.

If your emotions and feelings respond first for instance, then how can you mentally process the problem in order to determine your behavior? Use the space provided if required.

resources, volunteering your time, and engaging with others to complete goals. The common theme of these behaviors is helping. Prosocial behaviors can be positive in the sense that they replenish your energy levels and allow you to see the positive habits rather than just the ones that are negative. Being able to do this gives you an outsider's perspective and you're able to view your life from another point of view.

There is a certain **altruistic** nature about being prosocial, and this just means being helpful without expecting anything in return. Remember that this can be very negative if we are passive communicators and can't say "no". However, if you are struggling with making social connections, then this strategy can help break you out of fears that prevent you from engaging with others.

Ask yourself: *Do you have a fear of social situations? Do you tend to avoid interacting with other people?*

If you answered "yes", you are going to identify that as a problem and make the commitment to change your behavior.

Changing your behavior can appear as you putting yourself in a social or recreational situation that involves other people. Participate in activities involving the community or other social circles that you are or could be a part of.

Something to keep in mind: You want to get used to things that feel good, not things that feel bad. Just remember that most new things will feel weird at first, but the point is to release you from the

7

THIRD WAVE CBT

POSITIVE AFFIRMATION: With each new breath, I am growing stronger.

We've covered a lot so far and I know you've learned a lot. You should be proud of yourself. Now we're going to move into a range of CBT you're probably more familiar with in this day and age.

The "third wave" of CBT is considered to be one of the newest approaches and incorporates mindfulness and meditation. Both have an abundance of great benefits including the entrance of the theta alpha state which you will read about here in this chapter. The techniques you use in this chapter will also enable you to feel more relaxed and most importantly, more aware! This is because these techniques promote a higher sense of consciousness by forcing you to

mindful brings you into the moment. More and more it will help you to not get caught up in your thinking patterns.

Relaxation and Stress Reduction Techniques

Mindful **meditation** is simple: Focus on your breathing and how it feels in your body at that moment. Focusing on your breath produces that sense of calmness that makes us feel safe in our mind and body. Practicing these meditative techniques below will give you the skills that can help you lower your stress levels on your own! Doing so will allow you to gain more control of your own experiences instead of allowing your emotions to overpower you. These techniques can include: imagery, deep breathing exercises, and muscle relaxation to help center you and begin to relax.

- **Imagery Exercise**

Also known as *visualization,* imagery means imagining a scene that brings you a sense of calmness and release of anxiety. This is very similar to anchoring in that you are choosing an anchor, usually a scene, that allows you to feel more at peace in a moment of extreme distress. You can choose any scene that feels the most relaxing, such as a wilderness setting, perhaps somewhere you've camped.

This is most helpful when supplemented with some calming audio, like binaural beats!

Try This: As you inhale through your nose, count to four in your head. When you get to four, hold your breath for another four counts. Then exhale for another six counts and hold your breath again when you reach six. Exhale **completely***, when you can't push any more air out and vice versa.*

Imagine all the worries in your day exiting your body as you exhale.

If you're lying down, you can focus on filling your belly while inhaling, and dropping your belly while you exhale.

Practice breathing like this for five deep breaths.

3. Now broaden your focus to become aware of the sensations you feel, the sounds around you, and your thoughts that start floating on by.

4. Don't think about these ideas and external factors too much, you want to *observe* without placing judgment on them. If you feel your mind begin to drift from this moment, re-center by re-focusing on your breath.

- **Muscle Relaxation Exercise**

This technique involves tensing your muscles, so be cautious if you have chronic pain or muscle spasms.

You're going to begin with your feet and move all the way to your face.

1. First, take three deep breaths.
2. When you feel relaxed and calm, turn your attention to your toes. Imagine your deep breaths are flowing to your toes. Keep your attention here for about four or five seconds and then move your focus to the soles of your feet. Notice any sensations you feel in this part of your body and remember to keep focusing on your breath in your feet.
3. Then shift your attention to your ankles and repeat. Then focus on your calves, knees, thighs, and hips. Focus on these areas for at least a minute. Keep breathing, imaging your breath flowing to each part of your body as you move.
4. Move to your torso, lower back, and your abdomen. Feel your breath, see it flowing in your body.
5. Move to your upper back, chest, and then your shoulders. Notice any areas where you feel pain or tension.
6. Take three more deep breaths, see those breaths on your body, flowing with each inhale and exhale.
7. Good job! Notice how your body feels. It's always good to stretch afterwards!

Mindfulness can also come in the form of guided meditation for those people who have a hard time not wandering around on different topics as thoughts start floating by. These have been especially helpful for me because I am a very distracted person. So, trying to sit still and stay calm

ence **rapid eye movement (REM).** All five different waves are necessary for a full spectrum of brain activity.

There are two frequencies our brains work on, and those are **beta** and **alpha** waves.

Beta brain waves occur when there is the most electrical activity in our brain, and alpha waves operate at a slower frequency when there is less activity. This is understood as beta waves being of a low amplitude but high frequency and vice versa. "Where beta represents arousal, alpha represents non-arousal" (Scientific American). For example, beta waves would be occurring while we're giving a speech or performing in theater. The alpha state would occur when we're taking a casual stroll through the park or taking a small break during work.

Theta waves are on a lower end of the spectrum but not as low as **delta waves.** Both occur during sleep, but delta happens when we're in a *deep* sleep. We want to slow the speed of our thoughts but not fall asleep! This is why we want to be in the theta alpha state when practicing mindful meditation. We still want to be present, and a theta alpha state will allow us to do so while being in a relaxed state of mind. The theta alpha state is the state our brains are in when taking a nice hot shower. Have you ever noticed that you have a flow of deep, creative, outside the box thinking and new ideas pop up in the shower? To me the feeling is similar to the feeling during "Yin" at the end of "Vin Yin Yoga".

calmness that allows you to take a minute to assess the situation before reacting.

Brain Power

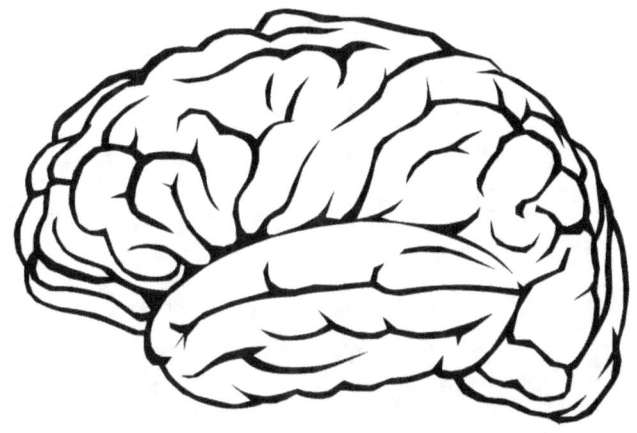

A study conducted by Dr. Dana Carney of Columbia University found that humans and other mammals' express power with open and expansive postures. Picture a "power stance" like the superman or superwoman pose: Open chest with your fists on your hips and your pelvis thrusted forward. The same goes for humans and mammals expressing powerlessness through closed, contractive postures. Studies have shown that "posing in high-power non-verbal displays (as opposed to low-power non-verbal displays) would cause neuroendocrine and behavioral changes" (Carney et al., 2010). This means that standing in an open position that promotes a feeling of power, doing this literally changes your brain chemistry. The feeling you derive with the pose

helps cope with adverse life events and recover with more motivation. Essentially gratitude promotes resiliency.

There have been studies proving that expressing gratitude at the brain level stems from the right anterior temporal cortex. This same study showed that a reason some people are more grateful than others is because of neurochemical differences in the **Central Nervous System** from their practices.

Founder of meditation training site, *Ziva*, Emily Fletcher categorizes gratitude as a natural antidepressant. This is because, "When we express gratitude and receive the same, our brain releases dopamine and serotonin, the two crucial neurotransmitters responsible for our positive emotions" (Chowdhury, 2022). These neurotransmitters make us feel good and immediately elevate our mood. Practicing gratitude strengthens our neural pathways making our internal brain functioning more positive in nature. By touching on the reward center in our brains, gratitude has a good effect on our subjective lenses.

In a study by Dr. Amit Kumar, participants were told to write notes to someone(s) that had a positive impact on their life such as teachers or friends. The notes had to be in-depth, meaning more than just a thank you. Kumar's study revealed that the participants, after writing their notes of gratitude, conveyed feelings of satisfaction in expressing their gratitude (Chowdhury, 2022).

Vision Boards

Vision boards can be a great tool for you to use to prime your mind to accomplish the things you truly want in life and reach your dreams. To put it simply, a vision board is basically a collage of images that represent what you want in life. You are conceptualizing the life you want. The purpose of a vision board is to serve as a motivator guiding you towards your dreams. People often refer to creating vision boards as being the same as *manifesting* the things you want in life. A woman mentor in my life uses vision boards often and she has a very clear picture of what she wants out of life as a result!

Now that you have all the tools and strategies in this chapter and the ones previous under your belt, in the next chapter you will learn how to set a goal plan for yourself.

8

SETTING GOALS

Positive Affirmation: I am working hard and something amazing is around the corner.

Since CBT is meant to help you become your own therapist, it's important to establish a plan for yourself to hold you accountable. Doing so gives you something tangible to work towards, and helps you stay on track. We've talked about having an intention and establishing what you want to achieve. We've talked about how to tackle your emotions and your cognitive and behavioral patterns. In this chapter, we'll talk more about how to solidify your intentions by setting a realistic goal plan for yourself.

Some people may find it too stressful in the beginning, which is why having a plan already laid out can be extremely beneficial. Remember that it takes time to adapt to a new

- *Who:* Who do you think needs to be present while you are working with a CBT practice? Or who needs to be absent.
- *What:* Get more specific by directly stating what you are trying to address with CBT.
- *When:* When will you start your practice (more in the "time-bound" section)?
- *Where:* This is not always relevant to an individual, but if it is, decide what location or setting is relevant to your practice.
- *Which:* Decide which things are going to be required of you or which things could get in the way of your goals.
- *Why:* Most importantly, why are you setting your goal?

Measurable: What will you use to measure your action steps and performance in meeting your goals?

Measurable refers to measuring your progress. What kind of metrics are you going to use to measure your performance and effort? This could mean writing in your journal every day, and you could use writing a thought record three times a day as the metric you use. This is a great way to figure out what could function as milestones for you.

For example: If your goal is to increase the amount of exercise you do, then you can measure your progress by committing to four days of running in the mornings. If your goal is to work on social anxi-

First of all, don't begin a CBT practice if it's not even something you can fit into your life in a manageable way. This just means that CBT isn't a process that can be rushed or done with little to no effort. We can all set a goal for ourselves but if the timing isn't realistic, you probably won't get the results that you expected to.

Establishing SMART goals will help you identify the specific areas you need help in. This works by helping you focus on what's important and what parts of your character deserve the most attention in your current life. When you're thinking of good goals to have, you can try this by examining what you want your goals to achieve. Consider your goals this way, do they:

- *Add* something to your life?
- *Enhance* something in your life?
- *Create* something for yourself?
- *Reduce* something in your life?
- Possibly even *preserve* something in your life?

If creating a goal list seems too daunting, confusing, or difficult, consider the behavior exercises that you learned about in Chapter 5. A few of them are meant to be executed in increments. You can apply that same method to your goal setting. It can help to establish your goals as you go, especially since sometimes, goals can change depending on your process.

CONCLUSION

Congratulations! You should be very proud of yourself. Notice any new thoughts and feelings you're experiencing now that you've reached the end of this workbook.

Cognitive Behavior Therapy *is* a psychological treatment, but that doesn't mean you need a therapist or a psychologist to practice it. CBT is for **anyone**, and anyone can do it!

I want you to think back to those three questions I asked you at the end of the Introduction:

What were your answers? Have they changed? Record your answers below.

    1. What core beliefs are you hoping to change with CBT?

✎...

2. What place do you hope to arrive at once you're able to learn these strategies?

✎...

3. Why do you want to change your thoughts and behavior?

✎...

Hopefully by this time you've been able to identify some core beliefs. Before we say goodbye to one another, we're going to go over some of the ideas we've covered and the types of strategies you can use to practice the new behaviors you've learned through each technique.

REVIEW

First, we know that we're all experiencing life according to our own core beliefs, which contain those absolute truths we've been conditioned to accept as fact. These absolute truths are present through our subjective lenses. It's these subjective lenses which influence our perceptions about the world and ourselves.

According to Aaron Beck's Cognitive Model, our subjective lens determines how we understand a situation. Based on this understanding, a situation will trigger automatic thoughts which then provoke specific emotional, behavioral, and physiological responses. Remember, it's our perceptions that decide how we feel, which is understood with the CBT Triangle.

How can we understand our core beliefs?

By locking the CBT Triangle in your head: Activating Events trigger our thoughts, emotions/feelings, and behaviors, and all influence each other.

The hardest part of changing our core beliefs is having to identify them and our cognitive distortions. What are your cognitive distortions?

- Black and White Thinking
- Catastrophizing
- Overgeneralization
- Muddy Filter
- Unqualifying
- Jumping the Gun
- Magnification or Minimization
- Emotional Facts
- "Should Have" Statements
- Labeling Lies
- Personalization

These cognitive distortions are what contribute to so many disorders and issues that people deal with on a daily basis— they're the traps that our mind creates due to the pain and trauma we have experienced. Cognitive distortions are huge red flags and can easily tell you that something in your cognitions needs to change. Starting with the beliefs that have solidified these distortions in the first place.

How can we go about tackling our cognitive distortions? Consider Maslow's Pyramid and The Franklin Reality Model. We as humans have a hierarchy of basic human needs that need to be satisfied if we are to continue to grow. We first must have that initial desire to grow as well to be able to efficiently locate false beliefs, otherwise it's all too easy to continue lying to ourselves about having a problem that needs fixing.

How do we know our basic human needs are being satisfied? Use the Reality Model to identify what principles are allowing or not allowing those needs to be met.

The strategies you can use during your CBT practice include:

- Anchoring
- Fact-Checking
- Thought Records
- Cognitive Restructuring
- Journaling
- Behavioral Experiments
- Self-Monitoring
- Exposure Therapy
- Activity Scheduling
- Role Playing
- Successive Approximation

- Shutting Up
- Problem-Solving
- Prosocial Activities
- Mindfulness Meditation
- Relaxation and Stress Reduction Techniques

All of the above will not only help you break your negative patterns of thoughts, feelings, and behaviors—they will also help you maintain the positive changes you make. Remember that any kind of therapy, not just CBT, requires consistency. In fact, making any new behavior of any kind won't become a habit unless enacted on a consistent basis. This also means *doing every part of* an exercise or skill too, because all are meant to work in conjunction with other methods of CBT.

For instance, meditating once may help you feel a little better in the moment, but unless you're practicing mindfulness daily, you're not going to reap many benefits. Another example would be practicing cognitive restructuring without writing anything down or keeping a thought record. Writing things down is a key component not just because it helps with memorizing, but it also helps you keep track of your behavior.

Many people won't need to try every single strategy and skill of CBT, such as someone with anger issues. Most likely that person may only try meditation or anchoring and not the other methods. That's okay; do whatever works for you, and don't push yourself to do things you aren't ready for. This is especially important to keep in mind because our traumas have existed in us for a long time, and force won't help us any quicker. In fact, forcing treatment could possibly have the opposite effect and may cause you to reject CBT or any other kind of therapy in the future.

When I first started practicing CBT strategies, I made the mistake of thinking that I was special. By that I mean that I decided knowing about CBT was good enough, because at least I knew *how* to get better.

But I didn't—and life taught me that lesson very quickly.

There is a prayer that is used in Recovery Communities called the Serenity Prayer, (Insert whatever higher power you believe in) "Grant me the Serenity to Accept the things I cannot change, the Courage to change the things I can, and the Wisdom to know the difference". See, you must have the Courage and Power to carry those things out because having the Wisdom just isn't enough.

Knowing you need help is not the same as getting it. Don't forget that healing first requires the desire to change, not just the knowledge. You have to *want* to get better, otherwise, you probably won't.

I want you to take with you this statement: *My thoughts are not facts, and all my problems have solutions.*

Not only that, but I want you to know that you're not alone. With continuous practice, CBT will change your life for the better, and for the long run. So above all, be willing, and practice, practice, practice! As I always say, practice makes progress. Be well my friends.

Watch your thoughts, they become your words; watch your words, they become your actions; watch your actions, they become your habits; watch your habits, they become your character; watch your character, it becomes your destiny.

— LAO TZU (TAO TE CHING)

A SPECIAL GIFT TO MY READERS!

Two Quick Hacks To Reframe Your Thoughts To Be More Positive!!!!

Included with your purchase of this book is your own copy of "Change Your Negative Core Beliefs, Find Your Hope" worksheets. These worksheets will assist you in digging into the very necessary work on yourself to gain a more positive outlook on your life. Improve your thinking and self-worth!

Scan the QR code below and let us know which email address to send it to.

For a supportive safe environment of like-minded people, join our CBT Mastermind Support Group on Facebook:

GLOSSARY

Attention Deficit Disorder (ADD/ADHD): a developmental disorder that is characterized by consistent symptoms of inattention (like being distracted, forgetful, disorganized, etc.) or hyperactivity and impulsivity (this includes fidgeting, interrupting, agitating, etc.). This disorder could also be shown with all three kinds of symptoms and isn't always caused by other problems and disorders, though that can apply to an individual as well.

Addiction: a compulsive, often chronic, mental and physical need for a substance and/or behavior, that has damaging mental, physical or social effects. Addiction is a disease that presents as habits that cause obvious symptoms like substance use, irritation, anxiety, distress, etc.). Some of these and other symptoms can worsen especially during withdrawal and early abstinence.

Affirmation: a positive assertion usually a positive phrase to lighten.

Aggressive: (aggression) tending toward or exhibiting aggression/marked by obtrusive energy and self-assertiveness.

Alpha Waves: an electrical rhythm of the brain with a frequency of approximately 8 to 13 cycles per second that is often associated with a state of wakeful relaxation.

Altruistic: having or showing an unselfish concern for the welfare of others.

Anchor: a reliable or principal to support.

Anchoring: to act or serve as an anchor for emotions.

Anger: an intense feeling of aggravation, irritation, hostility, etc.

Anxiety: a strong desire sometimes mixed with doubt, fear, or uneasiness/an abnormal and overwhelming sense of apprehension and fear often marked by physical signs (such as tension, sweating, and increased pulse rate), by doubt concerning the reality and nature of the threat, and by self-doubt about one's capacity to cope with it.

Anxiety Disorder: any of various disorders (such as panic disorder, obsessive-compulsive disorder, a phobia, or generalized anxiety disorder) in which anxiety is a predominant feature.

Apathy: lack of feeling or emotion/lack of interest or concern.

Arachnophobia: severe, or irrational fear of spiders.

Auditory: of, relating to, or experienced through hearing.

Autism Spectrum Disorders: Developmental disorders characterized by impairments in communication and social skills such as Asperger's and autism. These kinds of disorders are most noted by consistent behaviors and special, reduced interests.

Avoidance: an act or practice of avoiding or withdrawing from something.

Behavior: anything that an organism does involving action and response to stimulation.

Beta Waves: an electrical rhythm of the brain with a frequency of 13 to 30 cycles per second that is associated with normal conscious waking experience.

Bipolar Disorder: any kind of psychological mood disorder marked by alternating bouts of depression and/or mania.

Black and White Thinking: evaluating or viewing things as either all good or all bad.

Boundaries: anything referring to a person's limits or fixed borders around comfortability.

Central Nervous System (CNS): the section of nerve tissues that manage our sensory impulses. In vertebrates, the CNS carries the brain and spinal cord.

Cognitive Behavioral Therapy: talk therapy combining the cognitive with behavior therapy. This works by recognizing false patterns of thinking correlating with emotional and behavioral responses. The focus is on changing negative thought patterns to be helpful in order to produce positive emotions/feelings and behaviors.

Cognitive: in relation to conscious psychological activity i.e., reasoning, remembering, and thinking.

Communication: when information is exchanged between people through visual, written, verbal, and non-verbal kinds of behavior, signs, and/or symbols.

Conditioning: a simple form of learning involving the formation, strengthening, or weakening of an association between a stimulus and a response.

Elevated Cortisol Level: steroid hormones, also known as stress hormones, produced by the adrenal glands. When elevated, high cortisol levels can cause high blood pressure, weight gain, fatigue, and more. Cortisol can be helpful by providing anti-inflammatory and immunosuppressive bene-fits in addition to memory development and metabolism and blood sugar management.

Delta Waves: a high amplitude electrical rhythm of the brain with a low frequency of less than four cycles per second that occurs especially in slow-wave sleep, is most prominent in infancy and early childhood, and may exhibit abnormal activity in various conditions (such as traumatic brain injury or dementia)

Depression: a mood disorder that is marked by varying degrees of sadness, despair, and loneliness and that is typically accompanied by inactivity, guilt, loss of concentration, social withdrawal, sleep disturbances, and sometimes suicidal tendencies.

Diagnosis: the act of identifying any disease or disorder based on the symptoms done through examination/analysis in order to determine the root cause of the supposed condition or issue.

Dialectic: systematic reasoning, commentary or argument that compares contradictory ideas in order to arrive at a resolution or truth.

Distortions: the act of twisting or altering something out of its true, natural, or original state.

Eating Disorders: any kind of psychological disorder categorizing severe disturbances in eating patterns such as bulimia nervosa and anorexia.

Electroencephalogram (EEG): the tracing of brain waves made by an electroencephalograph.

Electromagnetic Radiation: a series of electromagnetic waves.

Emotion: a conscious mental response that is uniquely experienced as certain feelings toward an external or mental object or idea that is exhibited through changes in a person's physiology and behavior.

Encoding: to convert (something, such as a body of information) from one system of communication into another.

Exposure Therapy: psychotherapy that involves repeated real, visualized, or simulated exposure to or confrontation with a feared situation or object or a traumatic event or memory in order to achieve habituation and that is used especially in the treatment of post-traumatic stress disorder, anxiety disorder, or phobias.

Fear: an unfavorable, strong emotion produced by an awareness or expectation of danger.

Feeling: the one of the basic physical senses of which the skin contains the chief end organs and of which the sensations of touch and temperature are characteristic/the undifferentiated background of one's awareness considered apart from any identifiable sensation, perception, or thought.

Fight-Or-Flight: relating to, being, or causing physiological changes in the body (such as an increase in heart rate or dilation of bronchi) in response to stress.

Gaslighting: psychological manipulation of a person usually over an extended period of time that causes the victim to question the validity of their own thoughts, perception of reality, or memories and typically leads to confusion, loss of confidence and self-esteem, uncertainty of one's emotional or mental stability, and a dependency on the perpetrator.

Generalized Anxiety Disorder: an anxiety disorder set apart by excessive worry that is difficult to manage. Also known as GAD, it causes distress and/or consistent interruptions in daily activities and actions. This disorder is often the cause of panic attacks, disruptions in concentration, mood, sleep cycles, and more.

Genetic: relating to or determined by the origin, development, or causal antecedents of something/of, relating to, caused by, or controlled by genes.

Gratitude: the state of being grateful/appreciative of benefits received.

Grief: deep and profound sadness or suffering as a result of the death or loss of a loved one, relationship or anything else that was once held dear and can no longer exist.

Hippocampus: a curved elongated ridge that extends over the floor of the descending horn of each lateral ventricle of the brain, that consists of gray matter covered on the ventricular surface with white matter, and that is involved in forming, storing, and processing memory.

Image: visual representation of something.

Insomnia: abnormal inconsistency in sleep patterns where it's especially difficult to fall asleep and stay asleep.

Journaling: to enter or record daily thoughts, experiences, etc., in a journal.

Joy: the emotion yielded by pleasure, bliss, success, or as a result of the possibility of receiving desire.

Jumping the Gun: to make a hurried or prejudgment.

Kinesthetic: a sense mediated by receptors located in muscles, tendons, and joints and stimulated by bodily movements and tensions.

Major Depressive Disorder/Clinical Depression: a serious mood disorder involving one or more episodes of intense psychological depression or loss of interest or pleasure that lasts two or more weeks and is accompanied by irritability, fatigue, poor concentration, sleep disturbances, weight gain or loss, feelings of worthlessness or guilt, and sometimes suicidal tendencies.

Maladaptive: marked by poor or inadequate adaptation.

Meditating: entering a mental exercise wherein an individual practices control over their breathing and concentration in order to reach a higher level or awareness.

Mindfulness: the practice of consciously achieving a nonjudgmental state of awareness over one's cognition and emotions by being present in one's experiences moment by moment.

Monochromatism: complete color blindness in which all colors appear as shades of gray.

Mood Disorder: any of several psychological disorders (such as bipolar disorder, or major depressive disorder) characterized by abnormalities of emotional state.

Neurolinguistics: the study of the relationships between the human nervous system and language especially with respect to the correspondence between disorders of language and the nervous system.

Non-Verbal: (form of communication) not involving or using words.

Obsessive-Compulsive Disorder: a type of anxiety disorder marked by repeated obsessions and compulsions which cause tremendous distress. It's often very time-consuming and distracting, disrupting daily activity.

Olfactory: concerning the sense of smell.

Overgeneralization: to make excessively vague or general statements about something or someone.

Panic Disorder: an anxiety disorder characterized by recurrent unexpected panic attacks.

Passive: receiving or enduring without resistance/existing or occurring without being active, open, or direct.

Passive-Aggressive: conveying unassertive behavior shown through negative expressions of feelings, often due to resentment and aggression.

Persistent Depressive Disorder (Dysthymia): a mood disorder characterized by chronic mildly depressed or irritable mood often accompanied by other symptoms (such as eating and sleeping disturbances, fatigue, and poor self-esteem)

Phobia: an exaggerated and typically irrational fear of a specific idea or object such as Trypophobia, a fear of a small cluster of holes. The fear can also be of a certain situation, such as public speaking.

Post-Traumatic Stress Disorder (PTSD): a psychological response that arrives after an extremely distressing event or situation such as wartime or physical, mental, and verbal abuse. It's distinguished as flashbacks, depression, regular nightmares, etc.

Postpartum Depression: a mood disorder involving intense psychological depression that typically occurs within one month after giving birth, lasts more than two weeks, and is accompanied by other symptoms (such as social withdrawal, difficulty in bonding with the baby, and feelings of worthlessness or guilt)

Predisposition: (predispose) to make susceptible.

Problem-Solving: the process of arriving at a solution.

Procrastination: to intentionally, often habitually, postpone one's responsibilities.

Psychotic Depression: form of depression occurring when a chronically depressed person begins to experience psychosis. They are delusional and out of touch with reality. This is due to their brain irrationally processing information. This kind of depression is common in those with schizophrenia and anger issues.

Rapid Eye Movement (REM): a rapid conjugate movement of the eyes associated especially with REM sleep, or stage R sleep.

Rayleigh Scattering: scattering of light by particles small enough to render the effect selective so that different colors are deflected through different angles.

Reticular Activating System: a part of the reticular formation that extends from the brain stem to the midbrain and thalamus with connections distributed throughout the cerebral cortex and that controls the degree of activity of the central nervous system (as in maintaining sleep and wakefulness and in making transitions between the two states)

Retrieval: process of retrieving/to call to mind again.

Role Playing: to act out the role of/to represent in action.

Ruminating: to deeply contemplate something in the mind over and over to an excessive extent. This often occurs over a long period of time until the idea causes or is caused by harmful effects like social anxiety or depression.

Sadness: affected with or expressive of grief or unhappiness.

Schizophrenia: a mental illness depicted as interferences in cognition and behavior. It can appear as strong apathy, delusions, hallucinations or even appear as a lack of emotional responsiveness and recognizable declines in one's ability to function on a day-to-day basis.

Seasonal Affective Disorder (SAD): depression that tends to recur chiefly during the late fall and winter and is associated with shorter hours of daylight.

Sexual Disorder/Dysfunction: when an issue arises that prevents or inhibits the enjoyment of sexual activity.

Situation: an individual or combination of occurrences at a certain time.

Sleep Disorder: a medical problem that prevents a person from sleeping normally.

Social Anxiety: a form of anxiety that is brought about by social situations (such as meeting strangers, dating, or public speaking) in which embarrassment or a negative judgment by others may occur.

Stimulus Response: of, relating to, or being a reaction to a stimulus.

Stoicism: the philosophy of the Stoics.

Storage: the act of storing : the state of being stored/the safekeeping of goods in a depository (such as a warehouse)

Subjective: modified or affected by personal views, experience, or background/arising out of or identified by means of one's perception of one's own states and processes.

Therapy: (Therapeutic) producing a useful or favorable result or effect/having a beneficial effect on the body or mind.

Theta: (theta wave): a relatively high amplitude brain wave pattern between approximately four and nine hertz that is characteristic especially of the hippocampus.

Thought: an individual act or product of thinking/the intellectual product or the organized views and principles of a period, place, group, or individual.

Tinnitus: a sensation of noise (such as a ringing or roaring) that is typically caused by a bodily condition (such as a disturbance of the auditory nerve or wax in the ear) and usually is of the subjective form which can only be heard by the one affected.

Toxic Exposure: repeated exposure to a harmful substance over an extended period of time.

Trauma: a disordered psychic or behavioral state resulting from severe mental or emotional stress or physical injury.

Traumatic Brain Injury (TBI): an acquired brain injury brought on by an external force (such as a blow to the head sustained in a motor vehicle accident or fall or shrapnel or a bullet entering through the skull)

Trichotillomania: an abnormal desire to pull out one's hair.

Trigger: to cause a strong and typically negative emotional response/a person, place or thing that produces intense negative and unpleasant reactions.

Verbal: (form of communication) consisting of or using words only and not involving action.

Visual: (form of communication) attained or maintained by sight/producing mental images.

Written: (form of communication) made or done in writing.

REFERENCES

Aaron T. Beck, MD. (n.d.). Pearson Assessments. https://www.pearsonassessments.com/professional-assessments/products/authors/beck-aaron.html

Absolute truth. (n.d.). All About Philosophy. https://www.allaboutphilosophy.org/absolute-truth.htm

Acabchuk, R., & Vago, D. (2021, August 21). *Theta brainwave benefits: How and why to cultivate this mindful practice.* Round-Glass Living. https://living.round.glass/meditation/articles/theta-brainwave-benefits

Ackerman, C. E. (2022, January 26). *25 CBT techniques and worksheets for cognitive behavioral therapy.* PositivePsychology.Com. https://positivepsychology.com/cbt-cognitive-behavioral-therapy-techniques-worksheets/

Alvernia University. (2018, March 27). *4 types of communication styles.* https://online.alvernia.edu/articles/4-types-communication-styles/

Amen Clinics. (2018, May 15). *Where can you find help when you need to talk it out?* https://www.amenclinics.com/where-can-you-find-help-when-you-need-to-talk-it-out/

Amen, D., & Amen, T. (n.d.). *What your subconscious mind hears when you talk negatively to yourself.* The Brain Warrior's Way Podcast. https://brainwarriorswaypodcast.com/what-your-subconscious-mind-hears-when-you-talk-negatively-to-yourself/

American Psychiatric Association. (2020, December). *What is a substance use disorder?* https://www.psychiatry.org/patients-families/addiction/what-is-addiction

American Psychological Association. (2017, July). *What is cognitive behavioral therapy?* https://www.apa.org/ptsd-guideline/patients-and-families/cognitive-behavioral

Arguinchona, J. H., & Tadi, P. (2021, July 26). *Neuroanatomy, reticular activating system.* National Center for Biotechnology

Information. https://www.ncbi.nlm.nih.gov/books/NBK549835/

Arocho, J. (2015, November 23). *How CBT uses goal setting.* Manhattan Center for Cognitive Behavioral Therapy. https://www.manhattancbt.com/archives/544/cbt-uses-goal-setting/

Baton Rouge Behavioral Hospital. (2022, May 6). *Identifying emotional triggers and what they mean.* https://batonrougebehavioral.com/identifying-emotional-triggers-and-what-they-mean/

Beattie, M. (1990). *The language of letting go: Daily meditations on codependency.* Hazelden Publishing.
boom.boom. (n.d.). *How to use mental anchoring to reduce anxiety.* BoomBoom. https://boomboomnaturals.com/blogs/news/how-to-use-mental-anchoring-to-reduce-anxiety

Bruce, D. F. (2020, April 14). *Psychotic depression.* WebMD. https://www.webmd.com/depression/guide/psychotic-depression

Canfield, J. (n.d.). *Vision boards: How to create one & reach your dreams.* Jack Canfield Maximizing Your Potential. https://www.jackcanfield.com/blog/how-to-create-an-empowering-vision-book/#What_is_a_Vision_Board?

Carney, D. R., Cuddy, A. J. C., & Yap, A. J. (2010, October 21). *Power posing: brief nonverbal displays affect neuroendocrine levels and risk tolerance.* National Library of Medicine. https://pubmed.ncbi.nlm.nih.gov/20855902/

Chowdhury, M. R. (2022, February 5). *The neuroscience of gratitude and how It Affects anxiety & grief.* PositivePsychology.Com. https://positivepsychology.com/neuroscience-of-gratitude/

Christian, L. (2019, August 22). *The 4 communication styles: How behavioral traits affect communication.* SoulSalt. https://soulsalt.com/communication-style/

Cognitive Behavioral Therapy Los Angeles. (n.d.-a). *CBT for alcohol and drug problems: A 12-step alternative.* https://cogbtherapy.com/alcohol-and-drug-problems-los-angeles

Cognitive Behavioral Therapy Los Angeles. (n.d.-b). *Cognitive restructuring in Southern California including Los Angeles and Santa Monica.* https://cogbtherapy.com/cognitive-restructuring-los-angeles

Cognitive Behavioral Therapy Los Angeles. (n.d.-c). *How to stop ruminating | Clinically-proven rumination treatment Los Angeles.* https://cogbtherapy.com/stop-ruminating

Cognitive Behavioral Therapy Los Angeles. (n.d.-d). *Part 3:*

Applying the CBT model of emotions. https://cogbtherapy.com/cbt-model-of-emotions

Cognitive Behavioral Therapy Los Angeles. (n.d.-e). *Part 4: Cognitive behavioral therapy and mood.* https://cogbtherapy.com/cbt-emotions-and-mood

Cognitive Behavioral Therapy Los Angeles. (n.d.-f). *Part 5: Identifying automatic thoughts in CBT.* https://cogbtherapy.com/cbt-and-automatic-thoughts

Cognitive Behavioral Therapy Los Angeles. (n.d.-g). *Part 6: Cognitive restructuring to change your thinking.* https://cogbtherapy.com/cognitive-restructuring-in-cbt

Cognitive Behavioral Therapy Los Angeles. (n.d.-h). *Part 8: Opposite action, behavioral activation, and exposure.* https://cogbtherapy.com/opposite-action-behavioral-activation-and-exposure#

Cognitive Behavioral Therapy Los Angeles. (n.d.-i). *Problem-solving therapy in Southern California including Los Angeles and Santa Monica.* https://cogbtherapy.com/problem-solving-therapy-los-angeles

Cognitive behavioral therapy/Franklin reality model. (n.d.). Emergence. http://4emergence.com/evidence-based-practice/cognitive-behavioral-therapy

Crowe Associates. (n.d.). *Anchoring technique.* https://www.crowe-associates.co.uk/coaching-tools/nlp-anchoring-technique/

Davis, D. (2020, August 9). *Watch your thoughts.* Darryl Davis. https://darrylspeaks.com/watch-your-thoughts/

Davis, M. (2019, August 20). *8 ways to achieve self-actualization.* Big Think. https://bigthink.com/smart-skills/achieving-self-actualization/

Derby, F. (2020, October 30). *How to use CBT to manage fear.* Flourish Psychology. https://flourishpsychologynyc.com/how-to-use-cbt-to-manage-fear/

Echeburúa, E., & Corral, P. D. (1998). *Exposure therapy.* ScienceDirect. https://www.sciencedirect.com/topics/neuroscience/exposure-therapy

Ferguson, S., & Legg, T. (2019, February 1). *Catastrophizing: What you need to know to stop worrying.* Healthline. https://www.healthline.com/health/anxiety/catastrophizing

Galperin, S. (n.d.). *How to cultivate happiness with mindfulness meditation.* CBT Psychology for Personal Development. https://cbtpsychology.com/meditation-benefits/

Garcia-Rill, E. (2015). *Reticular activating system.* ScienceDi-

rect. https://www.sciencedirect.com/topics/veterinary-
science-and-veterinary-medicine/reticular-activating-
system

Hardy, B. (2020). *Personality isn't permanent: Break free from
self-limiting beliefs and rewrite your story.* Portfolio/Penguin.

Hartney, E., & Gans, S. (2021, November 13). *10 cognitive
distortions identified in CBT.* Verywellmind. https://www.
verywellmind.com/ten-cognitive-distortions-identified-in-
cbt-22412#toc-mental-filters

Harvard Health Publishing. (2021, March 17). *Two mindfulness meditation exercises to try.* https://www.health.harvard.
edu/alternative-and-integrative-health/two-mindfulness-
meditation-exercises-to-try

Hauser, E. (2022, January 11). *Here's why you remember things
better when you write them down.* LifeSavvy. https://www.
lifesavvy.com/19204/why-you-remember-things-better-
when-you-write-them-down/#autotoc_anchor_0

Hofmann, S. G., Asnaani, A., Vonk, I. J. J., Sawyer, A. T., &
Fang, A. (2014, January 8). *The efficacy of cognitive behavioral
therapy: A review of meta-analyses.* SpringerLink. https://link.
springer.com/article/10.1007/s10608-012-9476-1?error=
cookies_not_supported&code=70993d21-b0d5-4c08-af56-
1f45e554e1ed

Howes, R. (2017, November 30). *9 things you should know about cognitive behavioral therapy.* SELF. https://www.self.com/story/9-things-you-should-know-about-cognitive-behavioral-therapy

Johns Hopkins Medicine. (n.d.). *Chronic Pain.* https://www.hopkinsmedicine.org/health/conditions-and-diseases/chronic-pain

KASA Solutions. (n.d.). *What is the cognitive triangle and how is it used?* KASA. https://kasa-solutions.com/what-is-the-cognitive-triangle-and-how-is-it-used/

Keffer, L. (2019, April 1). *Absolute truth in a relativistic world.* Focus on the Family. https://www.focusonthefamily.com/church/absolute-truth/

King, L. (2019, November 15). *Who said your character is your destiny?* Medium. https://medium.com/mindset-matters/who-said-watch-your-thoughts-they-become-your-words-d645dff454b8

Kwik, J. (2020). *Limitless: Upgrade your brain, learn anything faster, and unlock your exceptional life.* Hay House.

Larson, J., & Biggers, A. (2020, July 1). *What is the purpose of theta brain waves?* Healthline. https://www.healthline.com/health/theta-waves

Mathews, J. (2015, December 6). *Stoicism and CBT: Is therapy a philosophical pursuit?* Virginia Counseling. https://www. vacounseling.com/stoicism-cbt/

Mcleod, S. (2020, December 29). *Maslow's hierarchy of needs.* Simply Psychology. https://www. simplypsychology.org/maslow.html

Merriam-Webster. (2016). *The Merriam-Webster Dictionary.* Merriam-Webster, Incorporated.

Metivier, A. (2022, March 17). *14 neurobic exercises for brain exercise and better memory.* Magnetic Memory Method. https://www.magneticmemorymethod.com/neurobics/

Morin, A., & Block, D. B. (2020, February 12). *How to perform behavioral experiments.* Verywellmind. https://www. verywellmind.com/how-to-perform-behavioral-experiments-4779864

Murphy, M. (2018, April 15). *Neuroscience explains why you need to write down your goals if you actually want to achieve them.* Forbes. https://www.forbes.com/sites/markmurphy/ 2018/04/15/neuroscience-explains-why-you-need-to-write-down-your-goals-if-you-actually-want-to-achieve-them/?sh=341a4a4b7905

National Institute of Mental Health. (2018, February).

Depression. https://www.nimh.nih.gov/health/topics/depression

National Institute of Mental Health. (2021, September 20). *Anxiety.* MedlinePlus. https://medlineplus.gov/anxiety.html

National Institutes of Mental Health. (2014, February 12). *What are the five major types of anxiety disorders?* U.S. Department of Health & Human Services. https://www.hhs.gov/answers/mental-health-and-substance-abuse/what-are-the-five-major-types-of-anxiety-disorders/index.html

New York State Department of Health. (2013, October). *What you know can help you - an introduction to toxic substances.* Department of Health. https://www.health.ny.gov/environmental/chemicals/toxic_substances.htm#:

Osadchey, S. L. (2018, August 3). *Somatic experiencing (SE).* GoodTherapy. https://www.goodtherapy.org/learn-about-therapy/types/somatic-experiencing

Peters, B., & Collins, R. (2020, August 5). *Reticular activating system and your sleep.* Verywellhealth. https://www.verywellhealth.com/definition-of-reticular-activating-system-3015376

Pietrangelo, A. (2017, December 5). *What is sexual dysfunc-*

tion? Healthline. https://www.healthline.com/health/what-sexual-dysfunction

Pietrangelo, A., & Legg, T. (2019, December 12). *9 CBT techniques for better mental health.* Healthline. https://www.healthline.com/health/cbt-techniques

Poepsel, D. L., & Schroeder, D. A. (2022). *Helping and prosocial behavior.* Noba. https://nobaproject.com/modules/helping-and-prosocial-behavior

Psychology Tools. (n.d.). *Behavioral experiment.* https://www.psychologytools.com/resource/behavioral-experiment/

Psychology Tools, Kaur, H., & Whalley, M. (2020, July 20). *How to use your CBT skills to conceptualize relationship and interpersonal problems: Two new formulations to integrate into your practice.* Psychology Tools. https://www.psychologytools.com/articles/how-to-use-your-cbt-skills-to-conceptualize-relationship-and-interpersonal-problems-two-new-formulations-to-integrate-into-your-practice/

Raypole, C., & Legg, T. J. (2020, February 27). *How somatic experiencing can help you process trauma.* Healthline. https://www.healthline.com/health/somatic-experiencing#uses

Raypole, C., & Litner, J. (2020, November 13). *How to identify and manage your emotional triggers.* Healthline. https://www.

healthline.com/health/mental-health/emotional-triggers#finding-yours

The Reality Model: These five steps will change how you act forever. (2015, January 27). The David Eccles School of Business. https://eccles.utah.edu/news/the-reality-model-these-five-steps-will-change-how-you-act-forever/

Reed, C. (n.d.). *How to change behavior with the reality model.* Colter Reed. https://colterreed.com/how-to-change-behavior-with-the-reality-model/

Ridgeview Hospital. (n.d.). *How to identify emotional triggers in 3 steps.* https://ridgeviewhospital.net/how-to-identify-emotional-triggers-in-3-steps/

Robinson, J. (2021, July 21). *Insomnia.* WebMD. https://www.webmd.com/sleep-disorders/insomnia-symptoms-and-causes

Robinson, L., Segal, R., Segal, J., & Smith, M. (2021, November). *Relaxation techniques for stress relief.* HelpGuide. https://www.helpguide.org/articles/stress/relaxation-techniques-for-stress-relief.htm

Rothstein, L., & Stromme, D. (n.d.). *RAS (Reticular activating system).* University of Minnesota Extension. https://extension.umn.edu/two-you-video-series/ras

Santos-Longhurst, A., & Ernst, H. (2018, August 31). *High cortisol symptoms: What do they mean?* Healthline. https://www.healthline.com/health/high-cortisol-symptoms

Scott, E., & Snyder, C. (2021, February 4). *Boundaries in relationships and stress.* Verywellmind. https://www.verywellmind.com/boundaries-in-relationships-and-stress-3144984

Self esteem (2014, August 21). Better health channel. https://www.betterhealth.vic.gov.au/health/healthyliving/self-esteem#characteristics-of-low-self-esteem

Setzer, L. (n.d.). *Experiencing objectivism through the reality model.* Rebirth of Reason. http://rebirthofreason.com/Articles/Setzer/Experiencing_Objectivism_through_the_Reality_Model.shtml

Sinha Clinic. (n.d.). *What are brainwaves?* https://www.sinhaclinic.com/what-are-brainwaves/

Stanborough, R. J., & Legg, T. J. (2019, December 18). *What are cognitive distortions and how can you change these thinking patterns?* Healthline. https://www.healthline.com/health/cognitive-distortions#personalization

Stöppler, M. C., & Ambardekar, N. (2022, January 22).

Progressive muscle relaxation for stress and insomnia. WebMD. https://www.webmd.com/sleep-disorders/muscle-relaxation-for-stress-insomnia

The Beck Institute for Cognitive Behavior Therapy. (n.d.-a). *Dr. Aaron T. Beck.* Beck Institute. https://beckinstitute.org/about/dr-aaron-beck/

The Beck Institute for Cognitive Behavior Therapy. (n.d.-b). *Introduction to CBT.* Beck Institute. https://beckinstitute.org/about/intro-to-cbt/

The Beck Institute for Cognitive Behavior Therapy. (n.d.-c). *Theory underlying CBT.* Beck Institute. https://beckinstitute.org/about/intro-to-cbt/

University of California. (2016–2017). *SMART goals: A how to guide.* https://www.ucop.edu/local-human-resources/_files/performance-appraisal/How%20to%20write%20SMART%20Goals%20v2.pdf

U.S. Department of Health & Human Services. (2022, March 1). *Depression.* MentalHealth.Gov. https://www.mentalhealth.gov/what-to-look-for/mood-disorders/depression

Valamis. (2021, January 19). *Types of communication.* https://www.valamis.com/hub/types-of-communication#verbal

Valamis. (2022, February 2). *Communication styles.* https:// www.valamis.com/hub/communication-styles#assertive

Vargas, P. T., & Yoon, S. (2004). *Encoding process.* ScienceDirect. https://www.sciencedirect.com/topics/psychology/ encoding-process

Watts, R. (2021). *Black and white thinking: 9 easy ways to stop for good.* Planning Mindfully. https://www. planningmindfully.com/black-and-white-thinking/

What is the function of the various brainwaves? (1997, December 22). Scientific American. https://www.scientificamerican. com/article/what-is-the-function-of-t-1997-12-22/

IMAGE REFERENCES

Clker-Free-Vector-Images. (n.d.). *Thinking person* [Graphic Image]. Pixabay. https://pixabay.com/vectors/thinker-thinking-person-idea-28741/

Johnson, G. (n.d.). *Brain mind* [Graphic Image]. Pixabay. https://pixabay.com/vectors/brain-mind-thinking-a-i-ai-2789698/